I would like to highly recommend Pastor Peter Tsukahira's book *My Father's Business* to all Christians and especially those who are working in the business field. This book will encourage you in your area of expertise—its message being that no matter what your calling may be, you can shine for Jesus Christ in that place. You may be the only aspect of Jesus that others see in the world, and your light can shine the brightest precisely where it is "business as usual." Please read this book to learn what Jesus meant when He said that He was about His Father's business. We all need to be about our Father's business as we follow Him.

— Dr. David Yonggi Cho
Senior Pastor, Yoido Full Gospel Church;
Chairman, Church Growth International

* * *

You hold in your hand a book that may alter your understanding of *"ministry"* and *"marketplace"* totally and for life. This is a well-written book by an author who is experienced and seasoned through a full involvement in all the dimensions of these two spheres. Peter makes complex elements easy to grasp, and, more importantly, he is teaching the truth. Some might argue that "something new" is being revealed here. It isn't that this truth is so new; biblical truth never is. What is new is that the subject is being dealt with in modern dimensions and presented clearly. This is a book I can recommend. Read it and digest it. It will be a rich source of blessing to your God-given ministry in professional life.

— J. Gunnar Olson
Chairman and Founder of
International Christian Chamber of Commerce

* * *

Peter Tsukahira lives in two cultures: church and business. This is not unlike the Apostle Paul and many of his contemporaries. Though Peter experienced some degree of frustration in earlier years trying to marry these two parts of his life, he finally realized that God had ordained it. He has become a strong advocate for what I would call apostolic leadership, not only in the church, but in the business community; these are men and women who are called of God to serve Him and become His representatives in the corporate world. Peter's book is wonderfully challenging to both cultures, business and church. The fact that he is an "Asian-American-Israeli" only enhances the message.

> — Rev. Don Finto
> Founder of "The Caleb Company"
> Former Senior Pastor, Belmont Church
> Nashville, Tennessee

MY FATHER'S BUSINESS

Guidelines for Ministry
in the Marketplace

By Peter Tsukahira

MY FATHER'S BUSINESS

Guidelines for Ministry in the Marketplace

By Peter Tsukahira

BRIDGE
LOGOS

Newberry, Florida 32669

Bridge-Logos
Newberry, Florida 32669 USA

My Father's Business
by Peter Tsukahira

Copyright ©2012 by Bridge-Logos
Reprint 2019

First Edition October 2000
Revised Second Edition August 2006
Copyright © 2006 by Peter Tsukahira

Library of Congress Catalog Card Number: 2012948017

International Standard Book Number: 978-0-88270-871-3

And He said to them,
"Why did you seek Me?
Did you not know
that I must be about
My Father's business?"
Luke 2:49

DEDICATION

This book is dedicated to my parents,

Dr. Toshio and Lilly Tsukahira

who built a love of truth into my childhood days,

and to my wife, Rita,

whose support and encouragement over the years

made it possible for this story

to be told.

CONTENTS

INTRODUCTION 13
    God's Rest and the "Rest of the Week"
    Salt and Light

PART I

CHAPTER 1: Launching Out.................................21
    My Journey
CHAPTER 2: Kingdom Professionals........................33
    The Apostle Paul's Model
    Kingdom Professionals' Model
    Ed's Story
    Bernard's Story
    Bettina's Story
CHAPTER 3: Giving to Caesar and to God.................47
    Creative Tension

PART II

CHAPTER 4: The Business of the Kingdom................61
CHAPTER 5: The Narrow Way 73
CHAPTER 6: Business with Missions 77
    Dwight's Example
    Don and Marlene's Story
    Bows and Arrows

INTRODUCTION

Galtronics
Opportunity International
Overseas Filipino Workers
CHAPTER 7: The Joseph Factor 87
Joseph's Success Factors

PART III

CHAPTER 8: Worship
    The Foundation for Business Success........................... 103
    The Business of True Worship
    Extreme Worship
    Great Worship
    Perfect Worship
CHAPTER 9: Integrity of Heart...................................... 115
CHAPTER 10: Focus and Singleness of Mind 123
CHAPTER 11: The Will to Win and Working Hard 127
CHAPTER 12: Resisting Intimidation 131
    Seeking Acceptance
    The Fear of Man
    The Power of God's Will
CHAPTER 13: Building Business Relationships...................... 135
    Managing Cultural Differences
CHAPTER 14: The Importance of New Beginnings............... 143

CHAPTER 15: The Priority of Prayer 151

PART IV

CHAPTER 16: Image and Idolatry 157
CHAPTER 17: Working While it is Still Day 167

Cases of massive corporate corruption have surfaced recently with disturbing regularity. The life savings of thousands of people have been wiped out or severely reduced by billion dollar scandals involving questionable financial reporting or outright fraud. Public trust in the "business as usual" status quo has been shaken. Increasingly, people of faith are being reminded that Satan is alive and well in the world of business. Trade and commerce have been his domain for ages. Many scholars believe that the description of the "king of Tyre" in Ezekiel's prophecy is really a description of the devil himself.

*You were perfect in your ways from the day you were created, till iniquity was found in you. **By the abundance of your trading you became filled with violence within, and you sinned;** therefore I cast you as a profane thing out of the mountain of God; and I destroyed you, O covering cherub, from the midst of the fiery stones.* (Ezekiel 28:15-16)

When Jesus was tempted by the devil, He did not dispute the evil one's claim to have authority over *"all the kingdoms of the world."* (Matthew 4:8-9) Satan offered these earthly domains to Jesus along with all their glory in exchange for worship. The Lord, whose kingdom is "not of this world," would worship only God. According to the Book of Revelation, at the end of time, Satan's representative—the Antichrist—will have authority over the world's financial system, and no one will be able to do business without his sign of approval.

*And he causes all, the small and the great, and the rich and the poor, and the free men and the slaves, to be given a mark on their right hand or on their forehead, and he provides that **no one will be able to buy or to sell, except the one who has the mark,** either the name of the beast or* *the number of his name.* (Revelation 13:16-17)

How, then, are believers—the children of God's Kingdom—to survive and advance in the world of business? Is this world redeemable according to God's plan? In past centuries, the Church has retreated from the spiritual battle over the soul of business. Many ministers decry the unrighteousness of Mammon from the safety of the church sanctuary, while others (also skirting the battle) shamelessly peddle the gospel to the highest bidder. The purpose of this book is to bring clarity to some of the issues facing believing men and women in business, and to help mobilize them for ministry, world evangelization, and the transformation of nations. In many churches, there is a strong belief that only full-time, fully supported ministers are truly qualified. One result of this deep but often unspoken belief is a "cultural gap" between business people and the pastors who serve them. Believers in business often feel misunderstood by congregational leadership. Although they may be very gifted in administrating or releasing funds for the work of the Lord, their potential for ministry is usually underestimated and underutilized. There needs to be an awareness of the fact that believing business people are a powerful resource waiting to be released for the building of the Kingdom of God. Ways to help business people find their spiritual calling and to train them creatively for the task defined by Jesus' Great Commission (see Matthew 28:18-20) must be found. An individual may be called by God to business but have a parallel call to ministry at home or on the mission field. Is it really possible for a Christian to succeed in business and ministry concurrently? Business and ministry may indeed require distinctly different skills, but integration is possible through proper training and discipleship. The purpose of this book is to bring this understanding of integration to believing business people and ministers alike.

God's Rest and the "Rest of the Week"

The integration of business and ministry is rooted in a Hebraic, biblical lifestyle. In his outstanding book on the Jewish roots of the Christian faith, *Our Father Abraham*, Marvin Wilson observes that Greek, Western thinking tends to divide the universe into two distinct parts: the material and the spiritual. This approach, known as dualism, stands in contrast to the Hebraic understanding that life is a dynamic unity and both the sacred and the secular are to be sanctified by God's presence. When God brought the people of Israel out of bondage in Egypt, they were not a nation in the normal sense. They had been slaves for four hundred years. They had no civil servants, no businessmen, no generals, and no formal social infrastructure. When they were with God in the Sinai desert, He spoke to them and promised He would make them a great nation that would be His example to all the peoples of the world. In order to accomplish this, God gave Israel His Law—the *Torah*—the five books of Moses. The Torah is far more than a religious manual or a guide to prayer. It clearly identifies sin as being that which is impure and displeasing to Him. The Torah also describes in detail what is pure and set apart for God in every aspect of life: dietary concerns, sanitation, national holidays, civil administration and justice, and even business ethics. It was all part of being a holy nation, destined for God's own purposes. In giving Israel such explicit commandments, God provided His chosen people with a complete culture in which to live.

This understanding of the "holy culture" God gave to His covenant people is relevant to believers today who are seeking integration of the sacred and the secular in their own lives. God's calls to business and to ministry may be equally holy in the life of a believer. He is clearly calling men and women to the marketplace and other areas of society—not just to pulpit ministries. When the church recognizes this fact and embraces it, the result can be the transformation of a culture. When we make a division between the secular and the sacred in our lives, we accentuate the "holiness" of our Sabbath day, and in contrast, we often let the rest of the week "go to the devil." We think of "the church" as being the place we go or the people we are with on this one day a week, rather than the *ekklesia* (New Testament Greek for "called out ones")—a holy people chosen for God's sovereign purposes. If we are to be a holy people and have every aspect of our lives submitted to God, the emphasis then shifts to the other six days of the week when we are called upon to demonstrate the kingdom's power in often corrupt and idolatrous surroundings.

Salt and Light

*Jesus taught His disciples, "**You are the salt of the earth; but if the salt loses its flavor, how shall it be seasoned?** It is then good for nothing but to be thrown out and trampled underfoot by men. **You are the light of the world.** A city that is set on a hill cannot be hidden. Nor do they light a lamp and put it under a basket, but on a lampstand, and it gives light to all who are in the house. Let your light so shine before men, that they may see your good works and glorify your Father in heaven."* (Matthew 5:13-16)

The Church must not allow itself to be confined to merely a Sunday activity led by professional ministers. Sabbath is a day of rest. It is a day for spiritual refreshing and renewal for the purpose of impacting the world with holy power during the rest of the week. Jesus asks, *"If the salt loses its flavor, how shall it be seasoned?"* What He means is that corrupt politicians will not reform corrupt politics, greedy businessmen will not change unethical business norms, and immoral pornographers will not voluntarily stop offering their filth to the public. The people of God are the "salt and light" of the Earth. There is no point in gathering on Sunday to complain about the sad state of our nation's politics, our economy, or our culture. If the Church does not work to change the status quo, it should not expect

PART I

change to take place.

A biblically integrated lifestyle is a radical seed for spiritual transformation in the marketplace, in government, and in the heart of cultures around the world. It is born-again business people, public servants, and believers in all walks of life who bring about this transformation by being obedient to their holy callings and producing good works. Jesus also said that if the salt loses its flavor, it will be good for nothing but to be thrown out and trampled under men's feet. Could it be that the failure of the Church to be salt and light in society results in believers being scorned and church involvement being considered little more than an uninteresting hobby? It is time for a radical re-examination of our biblical foundations.

There are places in the world where society is so dysfunctional that the Church can only pray. However, prayer mixed with faith and hope is powerful. Intercession is a mighty weapon from God in the hands of believers who are called and trained in its use. In fact, nothing will change until the Church begins to pray in earnest. However, intercession is just the first step. After evil principalities and spiritual powers in high places have been broken through prophetically inspired prayer, the people of God must be taught, mobilized, and sent out into society to fulfill their callings. Trained ministers are usually responsible for much of this process. The purpose is not to perpetuate and build the ministry, but rather to transform lives and impact the world. The producing of genuinely discipled lives is the heart of ministry and the key to the extension of God's Kingdom in this world.

It is God's intention for His Kingdom to impact and to ultimately transform all of human society. Jesus taught His disciples and every believer to pray, *"Your kingdom come. Your will be done on earth as it is in heaven."* In the very next verse, He taught us to pray, *"Give us this day our daily bread"* (Matthew 6:10-11). As much as we ought to trust God for our daily provision, we should also expect His Kingdom rule to be

CHAPTER

1

Launching Out

established on Earth. It is written in the Book of Revelation that when the seventh angel sounds his final trumpet, it will be proclaimed, *"The kingdoms of this world have become the kingdoms of our Lord and of His Christ, and He shall reign forever and ever!"* (Revelation 11:15). This is the Lord's ultimate purpose upon the Earth. Launching out as disciples of Jesus into the marketplace is an important way of participating in the Lord's eternal strategy for our world.

I groaned as I opened my eyes and rolled over in the pitch-black room. Somewhere an alarm was ringing and it was sending an unfamiliar message to my throbbing head. I again attempted to recall the events that had brought me to this foreign hotel room. The sounds from the people and the traffic outside my window reminded me that I was in a large Asian capital. I had checked into the hotel late at night after having arrived by taxi from the airport and I was due for an early morning appointment. I had been on the road for a month and I was exhausted. I had come to this particular city to finalize a deal with a new distributor for my company's products. Once in place, we would be in a position to bid on an important and lucrative government project. My position was Area Sales Manager for a company that made fiber optic communications equipment and my territory extended from New Zealand to Korea. This was the fifth country in four weeks and I had already stopped counting the number of business meetings I had attended. After I finished shaving, I knotted my tie and headed down to the coffee shop near the lobby. I was meeting the head of a local high-tech company for breakfast. Once business cards had been exchanged, breakfast served, and the expected pleasantries observed, the reason for the meeting was addressed.

"I know we can get the contract for you," the young company president asserted.

I looked at him intently. "How?" I asked.

"We are close to one of the decision-making officials," he said boldly, "and he has assured us that we will be favored because of our reputation."

"Okay," I said, "We'll send out a demo system as soon as possible and I'll fax you the forms to sign for your company to become our distributor."

It was raining during the taxi ride out to the airport and as I sat back and viewed the people hurrying by on bicycles and with their umbrellas, I began to wonder what exactly the company president had meant about "being close" to one of the decision makers. The sale would bring in more than half a million dollars for my company; however the end user was a government agency and any attempt to illegally influence the sale would cause us to forfeit the contract and result in a ban from further government business. My reputation would be hurt both in Asia and in my own company, whose headquarters were in the United States. How could I find out what was going on?

In the weeks to come, I questioned the president of our distributor by telephone and fax about the "close relationship" he had mentioned. At first he said simply that the person was a friend and then later he intimated that it was a family relationship. I knew personal relationships counted a great deal in Asia but I still sensed something was wrong. However, evidence to prove this was so seemed to be elusive. Then the president of another company that we had "jilted" in favor of our distributor called me at home. He was enraged and began accusing me of unfair tactics, vowing to do everything possible to defeat our bid for the project.

By the time the contract was to be awarded, I was almost sure our distributor was either paying one of the decision makers or had promised to recompense him later for information that would make ours the lowest offer. When the bids were opened, ours was clearly the lowest—except for one other tender. It was from the other company that had promised to defeat us. Their bid was less by an almost infinitesimal amount. Finally, the situation became clear to me. Our distributor had been cheating. He had accessed inside information to make our bid lower than the others, but our competitor had a better informant or perhaps had promised to pay the same person more! After months of work, we lost the project. I was devastated not only by the loss, but by the fact I had been unknowingly or half-knowingly involved in an unethical business deal that soiled my conscience and threatened my witness as being one who lived by biblical principles.

I cried out to God in prayer and repented for my laxity. I knew the Bible makes it very clear that God hates bribery and injustice. I had allowed the negotiations to proceed, thinking that ignorance would shield me from responsibility. I had sinned and I was sorry. Not only was I spiritually chastened, but I had lost a major contract and would suffer the earthly consequences. In the midst of my humiliation, however, I was inwardly relieved that we had not won unethically. We deserved to lose, and even though the competitor had also cheated, the outcome was just. It was a bitter lesson and one that left a lasting impression on me. God's justice is unwavering, yet, according to the Bible, His mercy triumphs over it. The story of this failed business deal, like many of the threads in the fabric of our lives, continued even after my stinging defeat.

Our competitor had contracted with a foreign supplier to manufacture equipment for the project. Three months later, they admitted they could not deliver the technology they had promised by the target date. They lost the project and were banned from government business for a period of time. Within a year, the same project was modified somewhat and reopened for bidding. By this time I had found another distributor who, although inexperienced with our technology, was trustworthy and efficient. This company had a good reputation with the government from previous work in other fields, and they won the contract for us with surprisingly little effort. When the equipment was successfully installed, I rejoiced not only at the unusual turn of events, but because of God's goodness. He had "resurrected" good business from total failure. In the process, I had received God's forgiveness and learned a valuable lesson about His character and my responsibility as a believing businessman.

My Journey

I am an Asian-American Israeli. I have an Asian face, an American voice and an Israeli passport. God has planted me and my family on Mount Carmel in the land of Israel. Since my wife, Rita, is from a Jewish family, we were able to come as *olim chadashim*—new immigrants. So we moved to Israel in 1987, became Israeli citizens, and began the difficult process of assimilating into a new culture, a challenge faced by first generation immigrants everywhere. When people look at me, they don't usually think I am an Israeli; however, I write as one who has made a lifetime commitment to this nation. Our daughter was two years old when we moved from Japan. She grew up in Israel, and is currently serving in the Israeli army. Our son was born in Haifa, attends public school, and will also serve in the army when he turns eighteen. Israel is our home, and we expect to live here until we die or the Lord returns.

My life was radically changed in 1973 when I had an encounter with the God of the Bible. At that time, Rita and I were part of the hippie counterculture. She came from the suburbs of New York, and I was born in Boston where my father was completing his doctorate at Harvard. During my early years, he taught Asian history at the University of California in Berkeley, and then, after joining the American State Department, he was sent as a diplomat to Japan. I spent my teenage years attending an international school in Tokyo, and returned to Boston in 1968 to enter university. In those chaotic years of the late 1960s and early 1970s, we searched for meaning in life in ways that were, many times, painful and even destructive. However, God, in His mercy, heard our cry for truth and brought us face to face with His reality. When we recognized that Jesus was truly the Messiah and Savior of the world, we abandoned whatever hopes or dreams we may have had about our own lives and said, "What is it that you want us to do? We are ready to go anywhere you want and do whatever you want us to do. We will speak whatever you give us to say. Here we are. Send us!"

Our lives have not followed a conventional pattern, in part because Rita is Jewish and also a believer in Jesus. Since the creation of the modern State of Israel in 1948, many Christians have had increased interest in the fulfillment of biblical prophecy. In the 1960s, a growing number of Jewish people began to believe in Jesus (or *Yeshua*, His Hebrew name, meaning salvation) as the Messiah. Messianic Jews mark a return to the origins of the New Testament community which was originally almost entirely Jewish. Their challenge today is to define, in modern terms, what it means to be both Jewish and a believer in Jesus the Messiah.

Both Rita and I knew that becoming followers of Jesus meant our whole lives would have to change. We grappled with our new identity as believers, and as we prayed and fasted, the Lord clearly told us to get married. In the very first weeks of our marriage, the Lord spoke again to me in, this time in an audible voice, and said, "I am calling you to serve Me in Japan and in Israel." This was a real surprise to us as we had no plans to move overseas nor did we have any idea how we might do so. We again prayed to know His direction and a short time later, the doors opened for us to go to Christ for the Nations Institute in Dallas, Texas, a school with a strong emphasis on both Israel and missions. We finished our two years of Bible training, and headed out to California where I entered seminary and began studying for a master's degree in divinity. One day, while driving to my uncle's home on the fourth of July, our car broke down on the highway and clouds of smoke began pouring out of the engine. It was one of those total breakdowns that I knew was going to require major car surgery. The car needed a new engine and we had no money to buy one. I was just an ex-hippie in seminary with very few work skills. I was taking a number of classes so I could finish my studies as quickly as possible, and was working as a bank teller in order to pay our rent and my tuition. We simply did not have the money to repair the car, so I was forced to borrow from a family member. It was an embarrassing situation and I began to cry out to the Lord in prayer for a better job.

Several months before this incident, I had prayed for

another student named Don who was in one of my counseling classes. He had worked for IBM before being called to seminary. Soon after our prayer together, he found a job with a minicomputer company run by Christians. There had been a revolution in the computer industry. Up until then, computers were huge machines kept in air-conditioned rooms and serviced by technicians in white lab coats. It was the mid-1970s, before there were personal computers, and this company was making state-of-the-art minicomputers. Compared to the computers of today, they were not small or even very powerful, but in those days, minicomputers were developing rapidly and being installed in many key industries. Don arranged for me to be hired on a trial basis. He said, "Peter, we'll give you ten weeks of training, and then you have six months. If you can prove you belong here, you can stay." I went to work learning to design and write programs in computer languages with strange names like COBOL and FORTRAN. Don, who was now my regional manager, came to me one day and said, "Peter, I had a vision of you. You were sitting at a computer terminal and everyone was crowding around you as you were showing them what you were doing." Now, this had to be a vision from the Lord because at the time I barely knew enough about computers to hold onto my job. But I discovered that I loved the technology. I really enjoyed the clean, unrelenting logic of computers. I was assigned to write a billing application program for a large corporate customer, Coca-Cola of Los Angeles.

Amazingly, my first COBOL program actually worked! Within two years I became a software instructor. I was beginning to teach computer programming languages and to design new courses. Don's vision had become reality. The company began to send me overseas to conduct training courses. After that, I became a junior marketing manager in this company, starting projects for new software products in different parts of the world. These projects continued to develop as my seminary studies were finishing. I received my degree and was ordained by the church. Rita finished her master's degree in communication and was teaching at California State University at Fullerton. I was on the staff of the church as an intern pastor. We were both enjoying our work, but we continued to look toward Japan because of the word that God had given us years before. In 1981, doors began to open to go to Japan. Rather than trying to raise support from different congregations, I realized that I had a valuable asset in my computer skills. I had worked in the industry for five years and had experience in several different departments. I sent out my resume to a number of different Japanese companies, and was eventually hired by the Japanese electronics giant, NEC Corporation. NEC actually interviewed and hired me in Massachusetts, but they promised to relocate us to their headquarters in Tokyo. After our move, I went to work in the heart of a totally Japanese company among 16,000 employees, designing and teaching software courses. I was thrilled to be able to introduce Rita to the city of Tokyo where I had lived as a teenager. The Japanese economy was booming and there seemed to be no end in sight to its growth. It was an exciting and challenging time to be there.

At NEC, we sat crammed into large open offices without partitions. I had a company lapel pin that identified me as an NEC man among the thousands of blue and gray suited men on the Tokyo subways. In the office, we listened to the company song in the morning and took a break for calisthenics at our desks in the afternoon. I lived a more or less typical *salaryman* existence. Rita taught communication theory in an international university. We knew God had brought us to Japan and knew He had other plans for us.

In our first week there, I was introduced to an American pastor who had recently established a fellowship for expatriates and English speaking Japanese in the center of Tokyo. Although we had expected to be involved in a totally Japanese congregation, it was clear that God was calling us to work alongside him. Bob, who had lived many years in Japan, recognized God's direction and invited me to be his associate. I was blessed to work with such a mature and experienced leader. He shared with me his vision for a large international congregation that would serve as an example of growth to Japanese pastors. However, Bob was also the regional director for his denomination and traveled frequently. I would pastor the congregation on my own for weeks, and sometimes months, at a time.

The number of people in attendance began to grow, and over the next few years, increased to over two hundred. Part of what drew people was the type of worship. We encouraged them to freely express their praise and love for the Lord. Aspects of Japanese society are very restrictive, and this freedom in the Spirit was exciting to young Japanese people. For them, experiencing complete liberty in worship and believing in the truth that sets human hearts free was radically life changing. At first we tried to find these new believers Japanese-language congregations near their homes, but eventually most of them remained in our congregation. Those were wonderful years for us. I took no salary for my pastoral work but was greatly fulfilled in seeing people from many nationalities getting healed and saved. At the same time, Rita's university students were coming to our home for study and discussion as we would examine life issues from the perspective of the Bible. During our years in Tokyo, dozens of students participated in these evenings and a number of them made genuine commitments to follow the Lord.

After two years, my employment contract was completed and I left NEC. I then worked for a well-known American computer company. They were opening up their subsidiary in Japan and hired me as their national marketing manager. I was responsible for their marketing programs, advertising, and new product promotions throughout the nation of Japan. As my responsibilities grew, I began to feel that my life was moving along two very different paths. Business and ministry were like the tracks of a railroad train. My life was the train. When the tracks ran parallel, I felt that the train gained momentum, and I could accomplish much. There were days when this dual track was exciting and even exhilarating. But there were other times when it seemed like the tracks diverged, when one side of my life began to pull against the other side. I was forced to make decisions about how I could limit one calling to allow the other to grow, and how much time or effort I could take from this one to allow the other to flourish. Our weekly pastors' meetings were held during breakfast at a hotel restaurant close to my office. I would meet people for pastoral counseling on my lunch hour. If people had to see me urgently, I would take a short break from my work and meet them in a local coffee shop. We would talk and pray, and then I would go back to my office.

My company's regional headquarters was in Hong Kong. One of my trips there was for a marketing meeting with the national managers from the entire Asian area. A yacht was rented for us, and we spent a leisurely day sailing out of Repulse Bay. By evening we had docked at an outlying island for a sumptuous seafood meal. The next night, the regional vice president invited me to play tennis. We played under the lights at his yacht club in Aberdeen. Afterward he said, "Why don't you consider moving to Hong Kong for six months and see how we do things in the regional office?" It was clearly an offer that would advance my career. I remembered a book on business success that stressed the importance of having a good relationship with your boss' boss. This vice president could put me in charge of a national operation! I thought of my own boss' beautiful home, his club memberships, and the company car with a driver that took him to work. As these images flashed through my mind, I knew what the answer had to be. I was a pastor of a congregation. It was impossible for me to leave Tokyo for six months. Then I had to figure out how to mask my disappointment, deal with my shame for feeling disappointed, and turn down the vice president in a tactful way.

There were times like these when, as a young pastor and businessman, I went through great frustration and a painful tearing process in my heart. There were moments when I asked the Lord, "Lord, are you ever going to allow me to really succeed in either one of these callings?" Sometimes I even asked God, "Would you please take me out of one or the other of these worlds?" I would argue with Him and say, "Lord, why can't I be like this minister?" or, "Why can't I be like that businessman? Why am I stuck between these two worlds?" I had dreams of succeeding as a minister and building a large, dynamic church. Japan was regarded as a "hard" field for the gospel. Less than 1 percent of the population were true Christians. A church of a thousand members, or close to it, would provide an example for other pastors. I wanted to be recognized for my spiritual gifting and respected by other ministers.

On the other hand, my business work required a lot of time and commitment. It not only paid my salary, but gave me the credibility in Japanese society I could never have as a missionary. Maybe God just wanted me to become a successful businessman. I could speak at luncheons and business forums and give the glory to God! But what about the church I was pastoring? With more than two hundred people, we weren't small anymore, and they needed me. I had Bible studies to prepare and teach, new believers to counsel, and sermons to give. I couldn't just stop being a pastor. Did the Lord want me to settle for mediocrity and obscurity in both fields?

Back in Hong Kong some months later and still wrestling with my dual calling, I went to a prayer breakfast one morning at the American Café in Wan Chai. I knew one of the men there, and after the meeting, poured out my heart to him.

"God doesn't want me to succeed," I said. "He has saddled me with two professions. I live in two worlds and I can't do it anymore. It's killing me. I want to quit."

"Let's have dinner tonight and talk about it," Bill said, and we agreed to meet later.

We had a meal that evening near my hotel in Causeway Bay, and Bill listened to all of my complaints. "Peter, God has placed you in the business world," he said finally.

2

Kingdom Professionals

"He doesn't have many men He can trust in business. You are there to reach people that will never otherwise be able to hear the gospel. Don't leave now."

I knew he was right. God was speaking to me through my friend. I went back to Japan encouraged to persevere, working for God in both worlds. The years passed and every time I hit a crisis regarding my dual callings, the Lord would send His Spirit to reason with me in prayer. He seemed to say, "Be patient. Stay put. You'll understand later. For now, endure the stress and allow your personal ambitions to die. Let Me work out your future." My dreams didn't die easily or quickly. But over the years, I learned that God is usually not so interested in what most of us define as success. What He considers success is to see us change. God is looking for transformation in the inner person—character change—not just adjustments in our outward behavior or appearance. As I struggled with these things my relationship with God deepened and my character was prepared for the challenges ahead.

I s it really possible to fully integrate the two worlds of business and ministry? Does Scripture define this integration as God's will? Many believing business people experience the personal stretching that I have felt, and wonder, as I did, how to find and stay focused upon Jesus' "narrow way" that leads to eternal life. I found I had to face that within me and the other Christians I knew, there existed a deep dichotomy between business and ministry. This deep division is found at the level of culture, my own culture and most places in the world that have been taught and discipled by western Christian thought. Culture contains values, perceptions, and expectations that lie beneath our conscious thoughts. Awareness of how one's culture affects every fiber of our being is a difficult process. In the past few years, I have been conducting cross-cultural training seminars for business people, primarily those in multinational companies, to help them understand the impact of culture on their interactions with colleagues of other ethnic and national backgrounds. As I seek to help people bridge the cultural gap in the workplace, I cannot help but see the tremendous need we have as believers to break down the cultural dichotomy between the business and church worlds. There is a church culture and there is business culture. Although the two coexist in the believing community, it is as if they have different values and goals, speak different languages, and have entirely different customs. There are variations by degree from country to country and from congregation to congregation but, in general, business and ministry are like oil and water. They just do not mix easily.

As a pastor, I recognize that business people have an important role in the congregational environment. They know how organizations work and they understand finance. It is good to have successful businessmen serving God and supporting the work of the church. But there seems to be an unwritten understanding that while believing businessmen support the work of the ministry, they are not to *do* the work of the ministry. On the other hand, ministers who preach the gospel

35

are expected to remain "unstained by the world" and out of the business environment. We try to keep these two vocations separate to prevent confusion, and, as a result, end up with a double standard in God's Kingdom. Rather than preventing confusion, this creates an artificial situation where Christians may be forced to forsake one of their callings so that they won't be torn apart by the opposing demands of two divergent identities.

From the church's point of view, business people tend to have a lower spiritual status. In certain countries this phenomenon is more noticeable than in other countries. It varies from place to place, but in general, businessmen are not considered to be on the same spiritual level as ordained ministers or pastors. At the same time, businessmen are thought to have more freedom and are not expected to maintain such a high level of sanctification as is required of ministers. They say in some parts of Asia that Christian businessmen have two pairs of shoes. When they get up on Sunday morning and it is time to go to church, they put on their "Christian" shoes. But when Monday morning comes and it is time to go to the office, they put on their "business" shoes. It is understood these are two completely separate worlds with different moral guidelines. This double moral standard does not exist in Scripture. It may exist in our society. It may even exist in our churches, but it is not consistent with the values of the Kingdom of God. I believe the Lord wants to eliminate the double standard and to break down this false dichotomy in the Kingdom of God.

I have been in Korea many times and recently the Christian business community was shaken throughout the country. The Korean church has experienced great revival, and there are many strong and vibrant congregations. Some of them are the largest churches in their denominations in the world. A leading Christian businessman, whose name is a household word in that nation and who was known for building some of the largest buildings in Seoul, as well as a church and Christian convention center, was sentenced to prison because of financial irregularities that were uncovered during a government probe of his business operations. I have heard it said by Korean Christians that this sincere, believing businessman did nothing different from what is done by the heads of many *chaebols* (business conglomerates) in Korea. However, the government made an example of him. He may have been targeted because the unbelieving world expects a higher level of business ethics in believing businessmen and their organizations than is found among nonbelievers. Ironically, the Church often holds the view that Christian businessmen can live with a lower level of sanctification than professional ministers of the gospel. There is no such double standard found in the Bible. God's process of sanctification takes place in the heart of a man or woman without regard to the work he or she does in the world.

The life of Jesus, our Master and Lord, exemplifies how one's business and one's ministry can be very much linked together. The gospels tell us that He worked in the business world. Some say He was a carpenter, but the Greek word is *tekton*, which simply means "builder." Studies show that He may have been a worker in stone as well as wood. He worked with His earthly father, Joseph, in the family business, which was what we would call today the construction industry. We know from the New Testament that He was a builder for more years than He was a minister. He spent eighteen years working under His father in and around Nazareth, and His public ministry lasted only about three and a half years. Many of Jesus' teachings and parables come directly out of the working world. He knew the lives of the people to whom He ministered. He knew what it was like for them to buy and sell. He knew the pressures and the temptations to compromise that faced them. He knew their hearts and their habits. This was because He had dealt with them in His trade for most of His life. In Jesus' case, we can say that business was His preparation for ministry. He labored patiently for many long years until the day came when He left the family business and never went back.

The Apostle Paul's Model

Another excellent example of someone whose work in his profession was concurrent with his ministry was Paul. Business was his vehicle for ministry. He was a skilled professional, an expert in his field. You never get the impression that Paul had trouble finding a job. Paul was a tentmaker. In those days, tents were not made in factories out of canvas or rip-stop nylon, but out of individual goat hairs woven together. In wet weather, goat hair swells up creating an effective shield against wind and rain. In hot and dry times, the goat hair weave "breathes," letting air and some sunlight through into the interior of the tent and making it cool and pleasant. Weaving tents was therefore exacting manual labor. It took a long time to master the proper technique, which was usually passed down from father to son.

Paul's tentmaking trade was highly mobile. Many people used tents in the Middle East so he was able to go from town to town and find employment wherever he went. Income from his work meant Paul did not need support from the local congregation. In fact, he boasted about this to the Corinthian church.

> *Do you not know that those who perform sacred services eat the food of the temple, and those who attend regularly to the altar have their share from the altar? So also the Lord directed those who proclaim the gospel to get their living from the gospel.* **But I have used none of these things.** *And I am not writing these things so that it will be done so in my case; for* **it would be better for me to die than have any man make my boast an empty one.** (1 Corinthians 9:13-15)

Paul was able to say to the congregation he planted, "I never burdened you financially, because the Lord gave me this tentmaking profession and led me to work with my own hands among you." Paul's work augmented and enabled his ministry.

Kingdom Professionals' Model

Jesus and Paul provide two good examples of those who did the "work of the Father" and also had experience in the business world; but there is a third model which suits most believers in business. I call this model the *kingdom professional*. A kingdom professional is someone who has integrated business with ministry and lives in both worlds simultaneously. In the Book of Acts, there is a wonderful example of a kingdom professional couple, Aquila and Priscilla.

Acts 18 records that during Paul's second missionary journey he came to the city of Corinth, an important commercial center on an isthmus with two seaports, Lechaeum and Cenchreae. In those days sea trade was predominant in the Mediterranean region and Corinth's ports controlled the trade on both the Ionian and Aegean seas. It was a strategically important city to plant a new congregation.

*After these things he Paul left Athens and went to Corinth. And he found a Jew named Aquila, a native of Pontus, having recently come from Italy with his wife Priscilla, because Claudius had commanded all the Jews to leave Rome. He came to them, and because he was of the same trade, **he stayed with them and they were working, for by trade they were tentmakers**. And he was reasoning in the synagogue every Sabbath and trying to persuade Jews and Greeks.* (Acts 18:1-4)

Paul first met Aquila and Priscilla in Corinth. Aquila was a Jew with an ongoing business in that busy metropolis. He was destined to become a biblical example of a businessman who launched successfully into international ministry. Interestingly, his name means "eagle" in Latin. Aquila and Priscilla hired

Paul, and they began working together in the marketplace. Paul went out every Sabbath to teach, and eventually planted a congregation in the city.

Acts 18 continues with the story of Aquila and Priscilla:

> *Paul, having remained many days longer, took leave of the brethren and put out to sea for Syria, **and with him were Priscilla and Aquila**. In Cenchrea he had his hair cut, for he was keeping a vow. They came to Ephesus, and he left them there. Now he himself entered the synagogue and reasoned with the Jews.* (Acts 18:18-19)

Paul stayed in Corinth for a while, working with Aquila and Priscilla in their established business. When Paul went back to his ministry base in Ephesus, Aquila and Priscilla went with him. If they were not believers when Paul first met them and began working with them, they were believers by the time he was ready to leave their city. They had caught his vision for missions, too, so they uprooted their business and moved. We do not know if they were able to transplant their tentmaking client base from Greece to present day Turkey, but they relocated to Ephesus and became part of the congregation there. What happened next to them?

> *Now a Jew named Apollos, an Alexandrian by birth, an eloquent man, came to Ephesus; and he was mighty in the Scriptures This man had been instructed in the way of the Lord; and being fervent in spirit, he was speaking and teaching accurately the things concerning Jesus, being acquainted only with the baptism of John; and he began to speak out boldly in the synagogue. But when Priscilla and Aquila heard him, **they took him aside and explained to him the way of God more accurately.*** (Acts 18:24-26)

Apollos was a gifted, Egyptian-born teacher. He was

mighty in the Word of God but not familiar with any baptism other than John the Baptist's. Aquila and Priscilla, however, had been discipled by Paul, so they took Apollos aside discreetly and instructed him more accurately. Apollos was not a "lightweight" in the ministry. In Paul's letter to the Corinthians he is mentioned in the same verse as Paul himself and the Apostle Peter. Some scholars believe that Apollos was the writer of the Book of Hebrews. Aquila and Priscilla, this kingdom professional couple, were led by the Lord to speak into the life of one of the leading ministers of their day. We can see their tact and sensitivity in not rebuking him publicly, which would have hurt both his work and theirs. They dealt with this well-known preacher privately and evidently influenced his life. Aquila and Priscilla were a business and ministry couple who matured spiritually as they followed God's call.

The story of Aquila and Priscilla does not end here. Their names appear a number of times in the New Testament, and notably among the salutations at the very end of the Book of Romans. Paul's letter to Rome is truly an amazing document. It is the fullest exposition of his theology and his understanding of God's purposes. It is an inspired message that looks down through the ages prophetically and still speaks to us today with life transforming power, as it has to believers for almost two thousand years. It foresees the calling of Jewish people to faith in Jesus and describes the place of Jews and Gentiles serving side by side in the Body of their Messiah.

*At the end of this powerful letter, Paul wrote, "Greet Prisca and Aquila, my fellow workers in Christ Jesus, **who for my life risked their own necks**, to whom not only do I give thanks, but also all the churches of the Gentiles; also **greet the church that is in their house**." (Romans 16:3-5a).*

What became of this business and ministry couple? They moved their business from Corinth and followed Paul to

Ephesus. They rubbed shoulders with the most capable and highly regarded leaders of the early church in that spiritually dynamic environment. Then they moved back to Rome, the great capital of the empire, and probably were successful in their trade and as outstanding ministry leaders. Paul obviously considered them among his closest friends and most trusted associates. Perhaps by the time they settled in Rome they were regarded as apostles, too. We cannot be sure of that, but we do know that this tentmaking couple became leaders in the Roman house church movement that challenged Caesar's imperial might and eventually outlasted it.

Aquila and Priscilla were kingdom professionals, and as such they can be models for us. We are not told that they left their profession in order to pursue the ministry. The Bible does not give us the sense that the early church saw a division between clergy and laymen or between business people and ministry leaders as we do today. All who believed were called to work out their own salvation with fear and trembling. Because the Church was more of a movement than an institution, there was far less reliance on position and professional qualifications. Greater importance was placed on calling and spiritual maturity. Anointed leaders exercised their gifts to edify the Church, and the technicalities of their support were worked out in the most practical way. Most of them worked in secular jobs.

I have been privileged to be acquainted with some modern examples of kingdom professionals.

Ed's Story

Ed is the president and one of the owners of a prosperous Chicago-based company that employs one hundred and twenty people and has an annual revenue of fifteen million dollars. His customers are in the farm equipment, automotive, plumbing fixtures, and construction industries. One time I visited him in Chicago. We wore hard hats as he showed me around a gleaming factory where state-of-the-art CNC machines were turning out precision parts of steel, brass, and aluminum. Some of his company's high-tech cutting tools are manufactured in Israel—a nation that has a special place in Ed's heart. He has visited there many times.

Ed is a kingdom professional. Aside from running a successful company, he and his wife, Cathi, are the founders and directors of a ministry that is pioneering a new concept in reaching young people with the gospel.

"Our core competency is ministering to young people," Ed explained. "When we began six years ago, there were hardly any youth churches in America. We started training young people to reach young people, and now we've become a model for other youth ministries around the country."

Ed and Cathi's ministry touches more than five hundred "at risk" teenagers every week in Chicago with high-energy outreach services, cell groups led by young people, ministry to addicts, college and career seminars, a coffee house, and a regular Christian concert ministry. In the last few years, they have been reaching out with love and encouragement to local teenagers in places as far away as Israel, Zimbabwe, Belgium, and Scandinavia.

"How do you handle the dual responsibility of being president of a manufacturing company in a competitive market, and being head of a growing youth ministry?" I asked him.

Ed answered, "A lot of people ask me that, and the key is that I'm committed to the team concept in both business and in ministry. In both areas I have a terrific team that is united in a common vision and purpose. That means I can utilize my time more effectively as an advisor or overseer. I put a lot of emphasis on training people. I try to get the right people into the right place at the right time, so that their gifts and motivations match our goals."

Ed has found many areas in business and ministry where there are crossover principles. Ministry experience and biblical concepts help him manage his business. For example, Ed looks for a positive heart attitude in the people around him and sees it as a requirement for success in the company, as well as in the youth ministry. Finding faithful men who will be able to teach others is a principle that works well in building a management team, although its original application is in disciple-making (see 2 Timothy 2:2). On the other hand, the business environment gives balance and healthy diversity to Ed's ministry calling. Spiritual work often seems to lack boundaries because it is based on qualities like faith, hope, and love that can be difficult to measure. The business world, on the other hand, has lots of structure. The constant necessity to manage time and other resources in order to meet clearly defined goals is good discipline.

According to Ed, many ministers could learn better ways of managing their time. He explained, "Business forces you to make clear decisions about your priorities and to avoid time wasters. Stockholders apply pressure on companies to grow every quarter, but there are a lot of ministries that haven't grown in a long time. The work of our ministry is rescuing young people and training them to live better lives. We want the ministry to grow while our business also expands each year. It's a goal that keeps us on our knees before the Lord." Other than receiving discipleship training from the Navigators in his early years, Ed has never been to Bible school or had any formal ministry training. Yet, Ed is the founder and head of a dynamic ministry and is considered an effective minister by many trained pastors. I asked Ed what he would say to other believing businessmen, and he answered, "Ministry should be an integral part of the life of every believer in business. You don't need another vacation home, another boat, an airplane, or another club membership. Get involved in what the Lord is doing. Start where you are right now and look for opportunities. Don't just give money, give of yourself. Unless everyone gets involved, we will never complete the Lord's work in our generation, and we will miss out on our own eternal rewards."

Bernard's Story

Bernard is a friend of Ed's in Chicago. He is also president and owner of a company that manufactures precision parts for the automotive industry. Bernard's company employs over two hundred workers and used to be located in the older industrial area of the city. After having moved his company to brand new facilities in 1994, Bernard was distressed to find fresh graffiti painted on previously clean walls nearby.

"I was angered and upset by the graffiti and looked for ways to stop it," shared Bernard. "Then I realized what needed to change were the hearts of the young people doing it. This led me to begin working to share the gospel with school-age kids. If the Lord can get a hold of lower income bracket kids before they leave junior high school, they have an excellent chance for the future. It's such an impressionable age."

Bernard established a center for after-school activities, and hired a professional manager to run it. He set up a board of directors and began channeling resources into the work. The result is a ministry that touches dozens of youngsters with sports and other character-building activities, along with the positive influence of the gospel. Some of Bernard's employees work at the center, too. It has been an inspiring challenge, and a deeply rewarding ministry for Bernard. He has continued to grow in his ministry calling.

Some years ago, Bernard and his wife Jeanne began visiting Israel. Their visits led them to a home for mentally disadvantaged children run by local Arab Christians in Bethlehem. Now this kingdom professional couple from Chicago are volunteering their time and energy to work with the children at the home. Sowing seeds of kindness and mercy are ways business people can begin to move into the flow of their ministry calling. None of this will go without reward from God. King Solomon in his wisdom wrote, *"Cast your bread on the surface of the waters, for you will find it after many days"* (Ecclesiastes 11:1).

Bettina's Story

In Manhattan's garment district, it was said that Bettina had the "biggest pencil on Seventh Avenue." As a top buyer for an internationally known fashion house, one order from her could make a garment manufacturer a wealthy man. She commanded an incredible salary loaded with perks that allowed her to travel the world and vacation virtually wherever her heart desired. She had worked her way up in the fashion industry and learned that hard work, attention to detail, and follow-up on business contacts were a necessity for success. Her natural gift for establishing and building personal relationships allowed her to win over some of the most difficult people in the industry. One day, however, Bettina encountered God in a powerful way that changed her life forever. She committed her life to the Lord and eventually found that the exciting world of fashion had lost its charm. Success, money, recognition and influence no longer gripped her attention as they once had. She began volunteering at a church that had just opened its doors in Manhattan's theater district. Soon she was administrating events and missions trips to various parts of the world. Bettina found the job skills she had developed in the business world could become holy instruments in His hand when she had fully committed them to the Lord's work.

Bettina discovered that God had used her experience in the business world to prepare her for the day when He would give her responsibility in His own "family business." By following the leading of God's Spirit, she became successful at administering and caring for God's own children, His Church. Today, Bettina is in charge of arranging events for one of the world's best- known evangelists and his team of ministers. Her ministry takes her all over the globe. The meetings she arranges now can involve thousands, and at least one time, close to one

3

Giving to Caesar
AND TO GOD

million people. For Bettina and so many others, business has been God's training school for successful ministry. However, instead of material success, their rewards are now eternal.

There are difficulties that occur when integrating business and ministry. Before a solution can be suggested, we must recognize the depth of the problem. Business and ministry are endeavors with very different cultures and definitions of success. It is not easy to function well in both of these worlds at the same time. No one will succeed in either business or ministry with a halfhearted effort. It often seems impossible to give sufficient amounts of mental concentration and wholehearted commitment to both business and ministry. The temptation to allow one calling to dominate and slowly kill the other, or to split the two and live a double life, is very great. Every believer in business will have his character and lifestyle called into question. Every minister who also pursues a business calling will be tested in the fire of criticism, inner questioning, and personal stress.

Thankfully, we have a great example in the life of our Master. Jesus maintained His integrity while being torn between His heavenly and human identity. His refusal to yield to Satan or to the public cost Him His life. Can we expect that it will cost us any less? The good news of the gospel is that, because of the Cross, the potential for us to follow Him and walk in wholeness has been preserved. Integrity in business and ministry is possible by faith—reliance on Jesus' sacrifice of His own life and His Resurrection from the dead. If we follow the callings God has chosen for us in the way He desires, ultimately we will not fail either as professional business people or as servants of the Most High God.

We should never trivialize the differences between business and ministry. They represent two divergent spheres of activity requiring very different sets of skills. For example, basketball and soccer are both games in which courage, determination, and sportsmanship are valued and rewarded. There is a level of excellence in which real champions of these games are recognized for their heart or character qualities. However, a player will never become a champion if he or she confuses the rules, skills, or required training of one game for the other. Business and ministry likewise have their own unique, practical guidelines that govern the way each must be pursued. Before we are able to integrate these two worlds, we must first recognize their differences and establish a theological foundation that is broad enough to support them.

In 1923, the American president, Calvin Coolidge said, "The primary business of America is business." What he meant was that the nation had a business culture, an orientation toward the marketplace that pervaded all levels of society. By and large, this is true of the United States and other industrialized countries today. But is this an appropriate or relevant way of thinking for people who are called by God to serve in the marketplace? President Coolidge's fiscal policies led America to a stock market boom in the 1920s followed by economic collapse. Does God himself conduct business? If so, what are the business policies the Lord has in His Kingdom?

The Old Testament Scriptures are consistent in their positive attitude toward commerce. Abram, a man of faith and referred to as God's friend, was *very rich in livestock, in silver and in gold*" (Genesis 13:2). With God-given wisdom, King Solomon conducted international trade, increased the wealth of his kingdom, and built God's Temple in Jerusalem. Inspired by the Holy Spirit, he wrote, "*It is the blessing of the Lord that makes rich, and He adds no sorrow to it*" (Proverbs 10:22). However, according to the Bible, all activities in the marketplace must conform to God's moral purpose for humankind. Amos, the prophet, spoke out against unfair taxation of the poor and the taking of bribes (see Amos 5:11-12). It is not wealth, but injustice, theft, and fraud, and gain by unfair advantage or by means of deception that God's Word condemns.

The New Testament does not introduce a bias against commerce. Instead, we are challenged with a deeper understanding of riches. True wealth is described as "heavenly treasure," and a crucial choice must be made between this wealth and the pursuit of earthly riches. At the age of twelve, Jesus said to His earthly father and mother, *"Did you not know that I must be about My Father's business?"* (Luke 2:49b). Obviously Jesus is not referring to His earthly father, Joseph, or to the construction industry. Jesus meant His heavenly Father and the business of building God's Kingdom. Luke's gospel goes on to record that Jesus' parents did not comprehend what He was talking about. Despite their lack of understanding, Jesus accompanied them back to their home in Nazareth and was obedient to them. As a builder's apprentice, Jesus probably made all kinds of things for the ordinary lives of His customers. Sinners contracted work from Jesus and His father, Joseph. The buyers did as they pleased with what they bought—for good or evil, for honor or dishonor. (Thankfully, nothing made by Jesus' hands is known to exist today. What an appalling religious idol would be made of it!) It is impossible to imagine Jesus doing shoddy work or cheating a customer on a bill or failing to pay the supplier of His materials on time. He surely was a good builder and an honest businessman. He paid His taxes and His tithe. He and His family must have been respected for the excellence of their work and the righteousness of their lives. Jesus intimately knew the daily routine of the working people to whom He ministered. He lived among them as a professional in His field. On the other hand, we have no record of any inspired words uttered by Him while He was a builder. Those years were His preparation for ministry.

In Luke 16, Jesus exhorts His disciples to be faithful first in their earthly businesses before God will entrust them with the business of the kingdom.

*He who is faithful in a very little thing is faithful also in much; and he who is unrighteous in a very little thing is unrighteous also in much. **Therefore if you have not been faithful in the use of unrighteous wealth, who will*** *entrust the true riches to you?* (Luke 16:10-11)

Many sincere believers in Jesus equate their work—their business in this world—with "the ministry" that God has given them. I believe this breeds confusion. Business is business and ministry is ministry. There is nothing wrong with believers conducting business in the world. Integration of business and ministry does not mean denial of their unique spheres. In a country where believers are harassed and even fired for their beliefs, someone once came to me and said, "I am torn between my deep desire to witness about my faith to my clients and my contractual responsibility to give them professional advice. Shouldn't I let my 'light shine' at work?" I told this person to give the professional advice with wisdom, honesty, and private prayer, and to witness after working hours to those clients with whom God gave him a personal relationship.

Some years ago while working at NEC, I met a young man who developed a great hunger for the Word of God. It seemed that every day at break time he would appear with more questions about the Bible. I greatly enjoyed trying to answer him, but I struggled to keep from being consistently late returning to my desk. After several months, I invited him to a restaurant after work for dinner. Before we even finished the meal, he prayed a genuine prayer of repentance and commitment to Jesus. Today, he is a pastor in Osaka. The boundary between the time for work and the time to witness is not always clear. However, if we seek to honor our commitment to our employer, there will be less opportunity for the devil to accuse us of irresponsibility, and we will have a stronger witness to co-workers.

John the Baptist preached repentance and holiness, but he did not demand his followers to leave their occupations even when they did work that was clearly of the world, such as gathering Roman taxes or serving in the Roman occupying military forces.

Some tax collectors also came to be baptized, and they said to him, "Teacher, what shall we do? He said to them, "Collect no more than what you have been ordered to." Some soldiers were questioning him, saying, "And what about us, what shall we do?" And he said to them, "Do not take money from anyone by force, or accuse anyone falsely, and be content with your wages." (Luke 3:12-14)

In His famous Sermon on the Mount, Jesus said, "*Let your light shine before men in such a way that they may see your good works, and glorify your Father who is in heaven*" (Matthew 5: 16). It is our "good works"—our professionalism, integrity, wisdom and success—that will win friends for the kingdom in the marketplace. People will be drawn to us when they see our good works. They will listen with interest to our words of faith when we describe a heavenly kingdom far greater and more real than this passing, earthly, economic city.

Jesus was both a builder's son and God's promised Messiah. He maintained absolute integrity in both callings yet He did not confuse the two. The possibility of any of us believing and being saved exists because one day, Jesus put down His familiar tools, left His place of work, and began to preach the Kingdom of God. The Bible records that "*Jesus was going throughout all Galilee, teaching in their synagogues, and proclaiming the gospel of the kingdom, and healing every kind of disease and every kind of sickness among the people*" (Matthew 4:23). Everyone who is born again has received a new life through complete identification with the death of Jesus on the Cross and His Resurrection. With Him we have passed from death into life, and in our new life, the Spirit of God is progressively transforming us into the image of Jesus. Our calling is to be like Him. Each one of us receives a measure of faith and spiritual gifting to accomplish our calling. Each one of us is given a portion of

Jesus' ministry by the Spirit. There is really only one ministry in which all believers participate as priests to some degree. It is the ministry of Jesus. He is our perfect Model and living Mentor for the business of the kingdom. The work of His ministry was comprised of prayer, teaching, preaching, prophesying, visiting others, healing, helping the hungry and poor, raising the dead, and giving himself as a sacrifice. All genuine ministry will incorporate or directly support these elements.

Some believers are called to full-time church ministry and are supported totally by the gifts of others. Most are called to earn a living and minister in a non-church environment. Employment in the marketplace for a believer can either be preparation for ministry, a vehicle for ministry, or both concurrently. Although Paul was a great apostle, he made tents commercially in order to support his disciple-making and church-planting ministry. We have no record that he preached the gospel while tentmaking, rather that he, after he put down his professional tools, went out to the synagogue or marketplace and shared the gospel of Jesus the Messiah. Some of Paul's spiritual illustrations were derived from his business experience. To the believers in Corinth, where he had worked with Aquila and Priscilla, he wrote,

> *"For we know that **if the earthly tent which is our house is torn down**, we have a building from God, a house not made with hands, eternal in the heavens. For indeed in this house we groan, longing to be clothed with our dwelling from heaven, inasmuch as we, having put it on, will not be found naked. For indeed **while we are in this tent**, we groan, being burdened, because we do not want to be unclothed, but to be clothed, in order that what is mortal may be swallowed up by life."* (2 Corinthians 5:1-4)

Tentmaking was not Paul's ministry but his vehicle for ministry. Followers of Jesus don't need to feel compelled to insert gospel tracts in every product they make, but every believing worker should feel compelled to strive for integrity and excellence on the job. Hard work and success in the marketplace give us the liberty to then offer the gospel to others, free of charge like Jesus did. In the same way that believing workers must strive for moral excellence in commerce, preachers of the Gospel of the Kingdom should never preach a gospel tainted with commercialism. We should preach the same gospel that Paul preached, a gospel devoid of financial promotion, self-aggrandizement or selfish ambition.

Paul said in 1 Thessalonians 2:9 and 2 Thessalonians 3:8, "For you recall, brethren, our labor and hardship, how working night and day so as not to be a burden to any of you, we proclaimed to you the gospel of God... nor did we eat anyone's bread without paying for it, **but with labor and hardship we kept working night and day so that we might not be a burden to any of you.** *"*

Business exists to provide value (products and services) to society. However, it must do so at a profit in order to continue its function and to grow. Harvey Mackay, a writer of bestselling books on business, once said, "There is only one reward the marketplace has to offer: money. If you're not making any, bail out. Quickly." Business in the world must involve making money. Kalyan Das of the Oxford Centre for Mission Studies told a group of aspiring kingdom professionals, "Making money cannot be the goal of your business. Making money is the *definition* of your business." For the believer, there is nothing wrong with making money, if this is his or her assignment from God.

It is written in the Psalms, "*The earth is the Lord's, and all it contains, the world, and those who dwell in it*" (Psalm 24:1). Thus, the creation of wealth is, in essence, the extraction of God's blessings that lie latent in His creation. Even the full-time minister who lives on the tithes and gifts of others must realize that it is fishing, farming, mining, manufacturing, and the profitable exchange of goods and services in the marketplace that somehow puts cash in the offering plate. We must work hard, trusting God to grant success, but we should not think that this business, which involves making money, is synonymous with our business in the kingdom. Professional success is a wonderful blessing from God, but His greater blessing is when we can leave our office and begin to minister the gospel free of earthly charge—for eternal reward.

This does not mean we cannot make money and minister concurrently. Like the Apostle Paul, we may work both in the business world and also for the Kingdom of God, as long as we understand that the two are essentially separate worlds. Jesus said, *"You cannot serve both God and money."* God is our only Master. He alone calls men and women to serve Him in various ways in earthly business and in spiritual ministry. God's blessing of success in business can provide opportunity to release time and resources to advance the Kingdom of God through the preaching of the gospel and making disciples.

Practically speaking, if you have adequate income and if you are confident about your reputation at work, you can take time off to go on a short- or long-term missions outreach, attend a Bible school, take gospel literature to a local prison, or begin a Bible study in your home. If you are an entrepreneur, pray about planting a business where it will benefit a mission outreach in another country. If you have a marketable skill that is mobile (like computer programming) you can look for a job in a company that will send you to a nation otherwise closed to the gospel. As an employee in a conventional company, seek to lead your co-workers to Jesus on your own time, not the company's, unless someone with sufficient authority asks you to preach to or testify at a company gathering. It is important to discern the difference between your earthly and heavenly pursuits and to *" . . . render unto Caesar the things which are Caesar's and unto God the things which are God's"* (Matthew 22:21).

Creative Tension

As someone growing up between cultures and living between two callings, I have had numerous occasions to experience the value of being stretched by God. Many times I thought I would break under the pressure, and just as many times, I was tempted to find some human way of escape. I found the only true and lasting release from this tension was in the comforting presence of God. Sometimes tension is caused by overwork, sin, or an imbalance in our lifestyles. However, tension in the life of a believer may also be caused by God's hand and be a part of His divine purposes.

A bowstring under tension releases energy to send an arrow to its mark. A concert violinist tightens her instrument's strings to a perfect pitch in order to play a beautiful solo. The tension created by opposing subatomic forces holds the matter of our universe together. Positive tension is an important part of human life. Spiritual tension also exists in a positive form. This kind of tension is best illustrated in the life of Jesus the Messiah. He was God incarnate in human flesh, all man and all God, yet perfectly whole. The life of Jesus was stretched between Heaven and Earth, connecting the two and defining the way, the truth, and the life for all who believe.

Handling tension creatively requires strength and endurance, yet from it flows power and productivity. There is a creative tension in business and finance. Keeping the flow of assets, expenses, and revenue in balance is a part of sound financial management and allows a good business to stay in business. Maintaining healthy financial ratios while maximizing income and minimizing expenses requires engineering positive financial tension within the whole system. Likewise, there should be a strong but positive tension between research and development (R & D) and sales. Salesmen want more features, faster delivery, and more advertising, while engineers need more time and resources to produce new products and features. Those who work in the financial department are always trying to minimize expenses. Creative leaders in business learn to use the tensions created by competing interests within the company to drive the enterprise forward.

There is an inherent tension between business and ministry. After His Resurrection, Jesus gave the command to all of His followers to make disciples of every nation. For this reason, every believer involved in business will somehow feel this pull between Heaven and the world. Business integrated with ministry in the modern world is a new paradigm that requires creative thinking and new keys of understanding from the Scriptures. Just as Jesus powerfully resolved the tension of His incarnation through His sacrificial death on the Cross and subsequent glorious Resurrection, believing businessmen and women must likewise resolve the tension of their dual calling through death to self-will while walking and working in the power of resurrection life. If our goal is to accomplish the Master's work here on Earth, we must sacrifice our own desires and will, and proclaim with Paul, *"I can do all things through Him who strengthens me."* (Philippians 4:13) In teaching about business and ministry, we should focus on integration without reducing the inherently different and often opposing forces in the two callings. Success in living an integrated lifestyle will produce great benefits for the gospel and also for us personally. However, standing in the creative tension requires spiritual strength, and it will cost us something in the process.

PART II

CHAPTER

4

The Business
OF THE KINGDOM

During the years that Rita and I were working and ministering in Japan, we knew we had a calling to serve in Israel. We had many Jewish and Israeli friends in Tokyo. Once again we found ourselves as a bridge between two worlds. Not only was I leading a congregation of Japanese and international believers in Tokyo, but we were also part of a community of Jewish people living and working in Japan. After five years in Japan we began seeking the Lord for specific guidance about Israel. We asked Him for confirmation and even put out some "fleeces." In 1987, the Lord opened the doors for us to move directly from Japan to Israel. We knew the time had come to leave and we believed God was saying to us, "Now is the time. I am calling you from Japan out of this congregation that you helped to build, and you are going to be a part of something new in Israel."

Knowing this was God's voice, we went. Again, it was business that provided the vehicle for us to go. I knew that the company I was working for in Japan did not have an operation in Israel, so I had gone to the Israeli embassy and asked their staff for a list of companies in the field of high-tech. They gave me a list, and I sent resumes to each address. One company replied positively saying, "We are looking for someone like you to develop our business in Asia. We want to meet you." We were not able to meet until about a year and a half later. But a meeting finally took place, and after some negotiations, the personnel manager said, "We're going to move you to the city of Haifa, and since your wife is Jewish, you need to come as immigrants. We'll take care of everything.

This company took us through the paperwork for making *aliyah*, which means "ascending or going up to Zion." In late December, as the heavy winter rains were falling, we moved to the city of Haifa. With the company's help, we found an apartment to rent on the top of Mt. Carmel, an actual mountain that extends several miles. This is the place described in 1 Kings 18 where the prophet Elijah confronted the false prophets of Baal. We marveled how God had moved us from Tokyo, one of the greatest business cities in the world, to the mountain of Elijah! For the next two years, I worked at setting up the Israeli company's business operations throughout East Asia. I traveled extensively because my territory included Australia and New Zealand. I actually saw more of Asia than when I lived in Japan because during our years there, my focus was almost exclusively on the Japanese market. Now I was dealing with an area at least twenty times that size.

In those first months, we felt the Lord leading us to put down roots in the society. I worked in a totally Israeli company. Saturday is the Sabbath day and Sunday is a working day in Israel. It is the first day of the workweek. Christmas is a non-event. It is business as usual. The beginning of the new year, celebrated the world over as New Year's Eve, is not a national holiday but something called "Sylvester" after a medieval Pope. Our new year, Rosh Hashanah, is taken from the Hebrew calendar and comes in the fall. My colleagues were secular Israelis who traveled as much as I did. Italy was a favored destination for a number of them. They loved the Italian climate, food and culture. Jokingly I would say, "When you are in Rome, don't forget to see the statues of the famous Israelis there." They would look at me strangely and I knew they were thinking, "David Ben Gurion? Moshe Dayan? Golda Meir?" So I would say, "Yes, there's even a huge, multi-billion dollar plaza in the center of Rome dedicated to a fisherman from the *Kinneret!*" (*Kinneret* is the Hebrew word for the Sea of Galilee.) Then my friends would be really puzzled. I would tell them I was referring to St. Peter's Basilica. I would then say what a shame it was that the Vatican had portrayed Jesus and His Jewish apostles as Gentiles and that they were no longer recognizable as the Jewish Israelis they were. At the same time, I knew that it is also sad that Jesus has been so rejected by the Jewish people that only a small minority of Israelis have ever read the New Testament—despite the fact that it is the single most influential book in the history of the world and was written almost entirely by Jews about Jews and events that took place in Israel!

God had placed in our hearts a desire to see a Messianic congregation birthed in Haifa but my long business trips abroad made it seem like an almost impossible dream. We also were not able to find the right people to partner with for this vision to take shape. The turning point came in 1991, at the time of the Gulf War. We had been in Israel three years and the impending war forced us to face some very serious issues. Saddam Hussein had promised that he would "burn half of Israel" with his missiles. We went ahead and prepared for his attacks, which meant getting our gas masks, sealing a room, and readying our children for the possibility of chemical or biological warfare. In the weeks prior to the Gulf War, one by one, the international airlines began to stop flying into Israel's Ben Gurion airport. They cited increased insurance costs as their reason for abandoning service to a country at risk. Most embassies withdrew their diplomatic staff to safer environments. Finally, the United Nations' peacekeeping forces sent their families home from Israeli cities. Facing the threat of a possible attack with biological weapons of mass destruction, those of us serving the Lord in Israel were forced to decide whether to stay or flee. Believers working in war-torn countries or in nations like Iraq and Saudi Arabia where expatriates have been the target of repeated terrorist attacks, must consider the same question. It is a decision that needs to be based on God's direct guidance rather than business concerns, family pressures, or personal safety. In the months preceding the war, we had to deal with our own fears, advice from family and friends to leave Israel, and even a very tempting offer to be transferred to my company's American office. But literally on the eve of the Gulf War, we made our decision to remain in Israel. Twenty-four hours later, in the middle of the night, we learned from a friend, who phoned from Florida, that CNN had just telecast the beginning of the bombardment of Baghdad.

In the end it was a very short war, and God miraculously protected Israel. Nine of the thirty-nine missiles that came into Israel were targeted for our city. The first night, a shopping mall that was under construction was hit by a missile, and for a time afterward it was known as "the scud mall." One missile did explode near our neighborhood, shaking the house and shattering windows several streets away. It was life-changing to go through a war experience, constantly aware that strangers hundreds of kilometers away wanted to kill us. Night after night, the alarm would sound as sat in our sealed room with our six year old daughter who was wearing her grotesque looking gas mask and our one year old son placed in a crib-like structure that was supposed to be impermeable to gas. We would read Psalm 121, reminding God of His words that *"He who guards Israel neither slumber nor sleeps."* He was faithful to His promise and protected His people.

Afterward, having gone through the war experience, we felt we had turned a corner in our lives as Israelis. Our roots had grown into the soil of our new country during those weeks.

Within a few months after the war's end, the Lord teamed us up with another couple who had come to Haifa to work with both Jewish and Arab drug addicts. David and Karen Davis had established a residential rehabilitation center, on the model of Teen Challenge. Soon after moving to Haifa, they met a number of believers in need of fellowship and teaching, and began a Bible study in their home. Rita and I heard about the group, and started to attend the meetings. Within a short time, we began praying together with them, "Lord, are you starting a new congregation?" Before long, the Lord answered us that indeed He was. So in June 1991, a new congregation was born, and I became a co-founder and one of the pastors.

After we had been pastoring *Kehilat HaCarmel* (Carmel Assembly) for several years, our leadership team was joined by another experienced minister and his wife who moved to Haifa from Jerusalem. Reuven brought with him a vision and burning passion for training others in discipleship. One of the first things he did was take our pastoral team through a series of teaching sessions in which he imparted to us the vision of disciple-making. It was a deep revelation. Before the series was finished, I was wondering, "This teaching is so central to the way Jesus taught. How could I have missed it?" The way I understood the ministry of Jesus began to change as I saw him continually turning away from the crowds while maintaining an intense focus on training His small group of twelve men.

If the business of the world is about making money, the business of God's Kingdom is about making disciples of Jesus. This call is described in the Great Commission.

*Jesus said, "All authority has been given to Me in heaven and on earth. **Go therefore and make disciples of all the nations**, baptizing them in the name of the Father and the Son and the Holy Spirit, teaching them to observe all that I commanded you; and lo, I am with you always, even to the end of the age." (Matthew 28:18-20)*

Although the long-term plan of Jesus' ministry was to bring about the salvation of the entire world, His attention was focused on these few faithful men. E. M. Bounds, who has written extensively on prayer, has rightly said that, "Men were His method." The production of men set apart for the service of God is the business of God's Kingdom. Oswald Chambers, the author of *My Utmost for His Highest* wrote, "God has only one intended destiny for mankind—holiness. His only goal is to produce saints." The glory of the Lord is shown in the fruitful lives of His disciples. In the business world, a company may have beautiful office buildings, powerful factories, and a smoothly operating financial system, but if these functions do not result in production, the company will soon have to shut its doors. The business of the kingdom is the production of discipled lives.

God wants men and women in every generation and from every tribe and tongue to be spiritually transformed. He wants their daily lives to shine with His holiness, His likeness, and image.

In Matthew 13, there is a very interesting account of one of Jesus' sermons that was given on the shores of the Sea of Galilee. Since this beautiful lake is only an hour's drive from our home on Mount Carmel, we have been there often. We know that perhaps two or three thousand people could stand along the gently curving shores and listen to someone speak without the aid of electronic amplification. The Book of Matthew records that Jesus got into a boat and pushed it a little way out from the shore so that all could see and hear Him. Since the crowd was full of local people from Capernaum, Tiberias, and the surrounding villages, it is probable that many of His own disciples' friends, family members, former employers, and neighbors were there. I think the disciples were hoping the Master would impress the people from their hometowns and that it might help explain to the skeptical ones why they had dropped everything to follow Him.

Jesus told a parable to the crowd that day about a sower, seeds, and different types of soil. After the teaching, the disciples asked Him, *"Why do You speak to them in parables?"* (Matthew 13:10). I think they were being very polite to their Master by asking in this way. It is clear that the crowd was not at all impressed with Jesus' sermon. The disciples may have been severely disappointed by the reaction of the people, and in fact, several in the crowd probably told the disciples they simply did not understand what Jesus was talking about. They had come to hear words of wisdom, and instead, what they heard sounded like an agricultural story.

Matthew tells us that Jesus gave the disciples this astounding reply:

> *"To you it has been granted to know the mysteries of the kingdom of heaven, but to them it has not been granted. For whoever has, to him more shall be given, and he will have an abundance; but whoever does not have, even what he has shall be taken away from him. Therefore I speak to them in parables; because while seeing they do not see, and while hearing they do not hear, nor do they understand."* (Matthew 13:11-13)

Jesus essentially said that the crowds were not able to understand. They had come to hear something exciting, to see miracles, or to eat free bread and fish, but ultimately, they would go back to their daily lives. They were interested enough to come to a meeting, but they would leave the moment persecution arose. At the end of the day, when the crowds had gone home, it was the disciples who would still be there with Jesus. It was to them and them alone that God desired to reveal His secrets.

Before He explained the meaning of His parables, Jesus said to His chosen disciples, *"But blessed are your eyes, because they see; and your ears, because they hear. For truly I say to you that many prophets and righteous men desired to see what you see, and did not see it and to hear what you hear, and did not hear it"* (Matthew 13:16-17).

Seeing this truth in the New Testament made me realize that a big difference exists between those who sit in the crowd and those who sit at the Master's feet. Disciples follow the Lord wherever He goes, even after the crowds go home. If we do not read the chapter carefully, we may think that everyone understood that the seed was the Word of God and that the soils were different kinds of hearts. It was not so. Jesus explained the parable of the sower only to the disciples privately. Therefore, the ministry to the crowd was a "sermon illustration" for the twelve. They must have realized that they had just witnessed the seed of God's Word being scattered over the ground, and that their own hearts were the *good soil* where the seed would grow and bear fruit. Much of our approach to ministry is just the reverse of Jesus' attitude toward His work. We want to minister to larger and larger groups of people and to a great extent measure the success of our efforts by the number of people attending our meetings. However, the preaching of the Kingdom of God is not about numbers of people; it is about producing disciples. We should always remember Jesus' command, *"Go therefore and make **disciples** of all the nations"* (Matthew 28:19a).

Many people call Chapter 17 of John's Gospel *the high priestly prayer* of Jesus, and so it is. However, I prefer to see it as our Lord's final performance report to His Father. In this great prayer, before He was taken into custody and ultimately to the Cross, Jesus prayed for himself, for His disciples, and for all believers. He said to the Father, *"I glorified You on the earth, having accomplished the work which You have given Me to do"* (John 17:4). What was the "accomplished work" to which Jesus referred? Salvation would be accomplished when He went to the Cross—an event that had not yet taken place—so the work spoken of in this prayer must be the changed lives of the men who had been given to Jesus by the Father.

Jesus is speaking almost exclusively about His own disciples to His Father in this great prayer: *"I have manifested Your name to the men whom You gave Me out of the world; they were Yours and You gave them to Me, and they have kept Your word. Now they have come to know that everything You have given Me is from You; for the words which You gave Me I have given to them; and they received them and truly understood that I came forth from You, and they believed that You sent Me"* (John 17:6-8).

Jesus did not pray here about the multitudes that followed Him, the finances of His ministry, the miracles of healing, or the feeding of the five thousand. His prayer was about His disciples. Then Jesus prayed for us and for all believers who follow in the footsteps of these men: *"I do not ask on behalf of these alone, but for those also who believe in Me through their word; that they may all be one; even as You, Father, are in Me and I in You, that they also may be in Us, so that the world may believe that You sent Me"* (John 17:20-21).

The number one requirement for success as a kingdom professional is radical discipleship. A disciple is someone whose heart and livelihood is fully yielded to the Lord's will. Even in the crowded marketplace, a disciple of the Lord is always with Him. When God calls men and women to business, He also commits Himself to always be with them. The challenge of the harvest in this generation must be met by businessmen and women who will answer the call to discipleship in their business lives. God's goal of sanctification is given to all of His servants regardless of their vocation. In fact, believing business people will face temptations to compromise their ethical standards that the average pastor does not face. Corruption in business is a fact of life. Business associates will offer bribes. There is a constant temptation to falsify financial reports on income to the government. After-hours "entertainment" offered by clients and superiors can put powerful pressure on believers in business to compromise their sexual purity. The average believing businessman or woman needs superior ethical standards and godly wisdom to function in the business world with excellence. God has too few servants in business that He can trust with large sums of money and the freedom to represent Him in a business environment, away from the watchful eyes of the believing community.

Church leaders can do much more to encourage and support the business people in their congregations. Recognition of the moral struggle and spiritual warfare that takes place in the workplace is a good starting point. A new vision is required to provide discipleship training specifically aimed at helping businessmen and women survive and thrive in the fiercely competitive corporate world. Business people should not look at their pastors and think, "That minister has a higher level of holiness and anointing than I will ever be required to attain." It is true that teachers of God's Word will be given a stricter judgment by the Lord. However, where does it say in the Bible that believing business people should not teach the Word of God? In many areas of the harvest today, it will be Christian businessmen who will open the doors of evangelism, long before there are any churches or church leaders available.

Discipleship for business people extends beyond simple sanctification. The real goal of discipleship is character growth through spiritual discipline. The Book of Proverbs states that, *"Poverty and shame will come to him who neglects discipline, but he who regards reproof will be honored"* (Proverbs 13:18). The business world offers a great challenge to believers to grow in faith and maturity through the daily moral testing that comes in the marketplace. However, it is important for believers in business who are launching out into ministry to find spiritual support and encouragement through close association with others like themselves. There is no substitute for personal relationships built on mutual trust between kingdom professionals. Spiritual accountability and transparency can provide the checks and balances needed for healthy spiritual growth.

As the ranks of kingdom professionals grow, specialized ministries are emerging to serve them and to help meet their spiritual and professional needs. One of the largest and best known networks for believers in business is the International Christian Chamber of Commerce (ICCC). The founder of ICCC, J. Gunnar Olson, began the organization in the mid-1980s as a platform from which the gospel message could be interpreted in a contemporary manner and proclaimed to the business world. His vision is for a worldwide network of committed business people in fellowship with one another, exchanging ideas, products and services, and helping to sustain and strengthen each other materially and spiritually. You can contact ICCC through their website: www.iccc.net.

A ministry also serving believers in a wide range of businesses, Marketplace Leaders, produces a daily e-mail devotional received by tens of thousands of subscribers. Founded by Os Hillman in 1996, Marketplace Leaders seeks to "help men and women identify and fulfill their God-given calling by applying biblical faith to their life and work." The ministry conducts workshops, consults with businesses and ministries and produces materials for churches and small groups. Os Hillman began developing Marketplace Leaders after a twenty-year career in marketing and advertising. He owned and operated his own ad agency and now uses the experience he gleaned in those days to mentor other Christians in the working world. In addition to working with individuals, he networks with other workplace ministries through the International Coalition of Workplace Ministries which holds annual summits for business leaders and pastors. You can tap into the resources offered by Marketplace Leaders by visiting their website: www.marketplaceleaders.org.

The Body of the Lord is like a fabric of interdependent lives woven closely together. We are incomplete without each other, and God desires us to function together in a coordinated unity. Some believers are called to spend most of their time in business in order to help support others who are being released for

CHAPTER

5

The Narrow Way

ministry. Some members of God's family are called to raise up
businesses that create wealth solely for the purpose of providing
employment and income for other believers. Cross-cultural
"business planters" and "tentmakers" are creating a modern
model for launching and sustaining outreaches that do not rely
on wealthy home congregations. Businesses that tithe their
revenue can support ministries of various kinds. In ways like
these, one person's gifting can be used to serve another person's
calling. This is proof of God's overall responsible management
and the dynamic economy of His Kingdom.

On either side of "the narrow way" of righteous business are traps that lie ready to snare a person and destroy his testimony in business. One trap is the failure to achieve business success and then camouflaging that failure by calling it "ministry." This is a deception. Many well-meaning businesspeople fall into other traps as they attempt to pursue success at the expense of biblical principles and personal spiritual growth. Often, the spiritual root of these errors is the sin of covetousness, wanting what the world has to offer. Hearts become focused more on the pursuit of money than on the call of God. The failure to deal with this as sin prevents the believer from breaking fleshly bondage to greed, and yielding to greed will destroy the believer's conscience, witness, and ultimately his effectiveness in the marketplace. Freedom from the spirit of greed protects a believing business person from *"walking in the counsel of the ungodly, nor standing in the path of sinners nor sitting in the seat of the scornful"* (Psalm 1:1). The blessing of the Lord is on the one who does not do these things. Psalm 1 goes on to promise that whatever such a person does will prosper. A blessed business person is not striving in the flesh, making costly mistakes, and breaking valuable relationships. He or she may therefore prosper in business through simple perseverance and faithfulness.

Covetousness is a sin of the heart that must die in order for the believer to succeed both as a business person and as a witness in his or her environment. The only solution for sin is identification with the Cross of Jesus. It is through deep moral struggle that we die to ourselves and rise again to new life in God's image. The Cross means the death of selfishness and pride as a motive for success in business. The price the believer pays for this kind of success is much higher than the price paid by worldly people. All citizens, both believers and unbelievers, are required to pay a percentage of their income to "Caesar" in the form of taxes. However, the believer needs to offer all his income to God and keep nothing except whatever God gives back to him for personal support and expanded service. If God were not a loving, kind, and benevolent Sovereign, this would seem like a cruel form of slavery. But because of His gracious character and His incredible love, this narrow way leads to success in business and great personal fulfillment. How many clever and gifted businessmen of the world have "gained the whole world and forfeited their soul"? In their hour of judgment, they will end up rendering everything to God they tried to selfishly keep for themselves, but it will not be enough, and it will be too late. This is not the inheritance of the believer in business.

John Porterfield is a Certified Public Accountant (CPA), who calls himself a "Great Commission Accountant." He tells this story about the practice of giving ten percent of our income to the Lord as a tithe: "A lot of believers think that giving a tithe of their income is all that they must do to please God. Imagine that I gave my daughter a shopping list for the family with ten dollars saying, 'Please go get these things.' What would you think if she gave me back one dollar and said, 'Get them yourself'? All of our money belongs to the Lord. We are His fiduciaries, that is, we have responsibility on His behalf for what passes through our hands. Many believers are 'embezzling' God's funds by acting as if ninety percent is totally for their own personal use." When we stand before God on the Day of Judgment, there may well be a moment when the books are opened and the angels will perform an audit in the sight of all!

Because of the narrowness of the way demanded by God, business for the believer cannot be merely a profession, but must be part of God's divine intention. The Lord has specific purposes and a life plan for every one of His children. Those who are called to business can expect His grace to always be sufficient for every struggle, storm, or crisis, but they must make their calling sure. It is important to periodically seek the Lord in concentrated prayer to confirm His calling to business. Every disciple of Jesus called to the business world should also remember that after eighteen years of success as a builder, one day Jesus left and never returned to that work.

It is the crucial power of the cleansing blood of Jesus that, through holiness, releases the energies, gifts, and talents that are hidden or latent in the life of the believer. This purity which is given by grace from God needs to be cherished and protected. Even though the Bible says, *"to the pure, all things are pure,"* (Titus 1:15) if a pure-hearted believer engages in sinful or immoral work, the result is that he or she will no longer be pure.

Jesus said:

> *Enter through the narrow gate; for the gate is wide and the way is broad that leads to destruction, and there are many who enter through it. **For the gate is small and the way is narrow that leads to life, and there are few who find it.*** (Matthew 7:13-14)

CHAPTER

6

Business with Missions

The concept of combining business with missions is not a new one. Some of the earliest Protestant missions were built upon a foundation that integrated business with the work of the ministry. In the days before the Industrial Revolution, skilled craftsmen were vital to the production of manufactured goods. During the eighteenth century, the Moravians sent numerous artisans abroad as missionaries. In the Americas, Africa, and Asia, the Moravians established an economic base for their ministry activities that also raised the standard of living in the countries to which they were called. Other mission-minded groups followed suit, and some of the fruit of their efforts survives to this day. William Danker's book *Profit For the Lord* documents the achievements of the Moravians, and tells the story of the Basel Mission Society of Switzerland who followed them in the early nineteenth century. Like the Moravians, the Swiss had a strong vision for business and missions working together. They established a trading company and sent skilled artisans to India. John Haller, a master weaver, developed the indigenous weaving industry there and also invented a new dye he called "khaki" after a local word that meant "dusty." The new dye was an immediate success, and was adopted by the Bangalore police as well as by the British forces in India. It is a color that is almost ubiquitous in the armed forces of the world today.

Napoleon once said, "An army travels on its stomach." God's army also has its financial supply lines, which often impose geographic limits on the spread of the gospel. Business, however, seems to be everywhere. With the spectacular rise of modern, global business as a feature of cultures around the world, believing business people have an opportunity to play a key role in the spread of the gospel. Business opportunities abound in many areas where the gospel has not yet made a permanent penetration. In addition to providing income for missionaries and local believers, a "planted" business demonstrates commitment and concern for the local people in a way often more easily understood than sermons. In some areas considered closed to the gospel, traditional forms of evangelism are simply not feasible. In many parts of the world the Church is exploding with growth, but in the non-Western world there are not enough funds in the Church to support those who are called to missions. Traditional methods of fully supported missionaries periodically leaving the field to raise funds from home churches will not meet the needs of today's harvest. Yet waiting until indigenous, non-Western churches are wealthy enough to fully support missions means losing precious time. New missions movements with church planters working together with cross-cultural business planters have shown they can create income in the very areas to which they are sent. By doing so, they can open closed doors and reduce the need for extensive, outside support networks. Missions in the form of profitable businesses may be the only practical way to develop lasting relationships with the local population and groups of indigenous believers.

Dwight's Example

Dwight is a man who lives and travels extensively in Asia. He calls himself a missionary, but his calling is planting factories. He has planted over ten factories in China. He is a skilled professional manager who worked many years for a well-known Fortune 500 company. He could easily command a six-figure salary from any one of many multinational manufacturing firms desiring to set up shop in China. He is an expert in planting factories, but where he prefers to plant them is among unreached people groups in that vast nation. The people that he chooses to hire as his general managers are born-again Christians. He looks for qualified professionals who have a burning desire in their hearts not only to build successful commercial enterprises, but also to raise up viable congregations for the Lord. He will only plant a factory in an area where the long-term goal is to plant a church. He told me about a factory he recently started in China. It is a factory that manufactures the small components for cellular telephones. It was a "green field" start-up, that is, an operation that was built from the ground up, from scratch. After word spread that hiring was going to begin, the best and the brightest young men and women from the entire region were lining up at the door to apply for jobs. He and his believing managers had their pick of the most promising young people in that area. Once hired, they would not only learn skills in high technology manufacturing, but would also be exposed to the gospel of Jesus Christ.

One of the important advantages of business being integrated with missions in an underdeveloped area is that new jobs are created. This raises the standard of living for the very people being reached with the gospel and reduces the resentment so often felt by locals toward missionaries supported from outside who live at a higher economic level than those around them. Business combined with missions can create income, build up the daily lives of the local people, while demonstrating to them the reality of the gospel message. The potential of this new paradigm in missions has attracted the attention of some large and established mission agencies around the world. They are beginning to experiment with new ways of releasing qualified kingdom professionals into the harvest fields of the world.

Don and Marlene's Story

Don and Marlene's life story does not follow a conventional pattern. Brought up in strong Christian families, they remember a time when wealth was considered worldly, and it seemed wrong for real Christians to have money. As a young man, Don studied for the ministry and was ordained. He and Marlene were married and launched out as missionaries to the Philippines in 1958. Their missionary calling led them to Davao, a city in the southern Philippines, where they began preaching the gospel and eventually succeeded in planting a single, small church. A few young and promising Filipinos came to the Lord and Don poured his heart into teaching them to be disciples. One of these young men, Augustine, showed particular promise and Don helped him through some difficult times as he grew in his faith.

Three years after beginning their work in the Philippines, Marlene's father and sister were killed in an airplane crash. Don and Marlene were called back to the United States where they assumed responsibility for Marlene's father's business. He had operated a small chain of nursing homes. Business was the last thing Don wanted to do. He believed being a businessman was spiritually a step down from serving the Lord on the mission field. Out of a sense of obligation to the family, he grudgingly "put his hand to the plow" and began trying to administer the business. It was extremely hard. The existing nursing homes were in buildings rented from the county and some were unable to meet local fire codes. Moreover, Don's heart simply was not in it. He struggled on month after month while a number of experienced managers left. One day, another minister, after listening to Don's litany of complaints, could no longer hold his peace. "Don," he burst out, "God has put you here. You have got to run this business!" Realizing the truth of these words, Don began to apply himself to improving the nursing homes, building new facilities, and getting them on a sound financial foundation. He employed biblical principles in his management style and God blessed his efforts with unusual favor. The business began to prosper.

Inwardly, Don had a problem with his identity. Was he a preacher or a businessman? Since childhood he had believed that money would destroy his spiritual life, and he was afraid of succumbing to the temptations of material wealth. As he prayed, God seemed to say, "Son, it makes no difference what men call you. Just do my will and bring glory to my name!" He was influenced by the preaching of T.L. Osborne and began to see how business could help reach the world with the gospel. Don began to get a vision of how he could serve the Kingdom of God as a businessman.

In the meantime, Don visited the Philippines every year. He began to bring with him powerful Christian teachers who inspired his small flock and built up their faith to believe God for miracles. Because of Don's input and the help of others, the congregation was growing. Don's disciple, Augustine, a former accountant, emerged as a gifted pastor as well as a man of wisdom and integrity. He applied his skill with figures as well as his own high ethical standards to managing the funds being funneled into the work of the church from Don's growing business.

Over a period of several decades, Don and Marlene have seen God move in a tremendous way. Their business grew to include nursing homes in several states resulting in annual revenue in the millions. They provide high quality care, and their occupancy rates are consistently more than 10 percent above the national average. Many of their key managers have been with them for twenty years or more. Recently, their oldest son was named company president, and the business is poised for further growth.

In the Philippines, the first congregation they planted has grown steadily and multiplied by discipling and sending out young leaders. Now a network of over 500 churches trace their roots back to the original congregation Don and Marlene planted. These churches touch the lives of thousands of people on a regular basis. Don still ministers among them on his annual visits, more than forty years later.

"If we hadn't accepted God's direction into business back then, none of this could ever have happened," Don said recently. "It takes resources to move God's Kingdom forward. As business people we had the money to bring high quality ministers to our people in the field and to help them buy needed equipment. We taught them to exercise their own faith to grow their ministries."

Don and Marlene's hearts have always been committed to building God's heavenly Kingdom, but their day to day business required a focus on the here and now. People still aren't sure what to call them. Are they business people or are they missionaries? I asked them what the main factor was that led to their success as kingdom professionals. They replied, "Giving is the key. If you have the faith to give in obedience to the Lord, He will bless you with more and more. We always tithed on our business income and looked for opportunities to be generous. We were not trained business people but faith and obedience to God helped us fulfill His calling. Along the way, God told us to give away some very expensive things, but He always gave us back more than we expected. We have seen more than our share of miracles."

Today, Don and Marlene are financially able to travel and minister in many countries. They are strong supporters of their local church and organize business forums and seminars. Their lives and career serve as an example for many younger Christians launching out into business and ministry. Like many other kingdom professionals, Don and Marlene still wear two hats all the time.

Bows and Arrows

Christians are reaching out in numerous ways to developing countries using business as their vehicle. Another example of this is a group of companies that use a bow and arrow as their motif. Their concept encompasses "bow" companies that produce revenue for launching outreaches and "arrow" companies that are sent out for the Lord's purposes. This innovative organization builds and nurtures businesses that can penetrate areas otherwise closed to the gospel. It is based in Singapore and is involved in a variety of Great Commission-oriented ventures including consulting, franchising, and human resource management. Among these ventures is a business planted in neighboring Cambodia that exports local handicrafts to markets in London and other cities. Upscale shops selling exotic handmade household furnishings to affluent Westerners are providing income for local artisans and believers. Volunteers from abroad have come alongside to mentor and disciple the Christian employees. Another related business in Cambodia employs the graduates of a planted engineering vocational training program. All of these graduates are orphans and former street kids who are now Christians. They are going beyond the level of industrial apprentices and are learning skills that will, in time, help them to manage their own businesses.

Galtronics

Galtronics is a company in Israel making wireless communications equipment. It was started by a Christian businessman a number of years ago. Ken, the founder of the company, was a young engineer when God spoke to him and his wife to come to Israel and help God's covenant people, the Jews. Established mission agencies were not able to send them but they came to Israel anyway and began a small factory near the Sea of Galilee making antennas for walkie-talkies. The early years were very hard for them, and they weathered numerous difficulties in starting up the business. They also received physical attacks from ultra-orthodox Jewish groups who questioned their motives and objected to their presence in the city. In the end, they succeeded in hiring a few people and establishing a viable small business. Then the worldwide cellular telephone boom hit. Demand for small antennas skyrocketed, and the company was ideally positioned to participate in the growth.

Now Galtronics is the third largest supplier of cellular phone antennas in the world. They market their products worldwide and hold a number of key patents in the field. They are the largest employer in their city, and are winners of the Kaplan Prize, Israel's top industrial prize. They have always been open about their identity as a believing company and have been instrumental in planting an indigenous Messianic congregation in their city. Today this congregation is one of the largest Hebrew-speaking congregations in Israel.

I remember well the effect this company had on the entire Israeli electronics industry. The fiber optics company I worked for when we first moved to Israel won an industrial prize the same year as Ken's company. That year the Minister of Industry and Trade was an ultra-orthodox rabbi whose last name, *Porush*, literally means Pharisee in Hebrew. He objected to the fact that believers in *Yeshua* (Hebrew for Jesus) had won the prize. It was his job to hand the certificate to the winning executives and shake their hands, but he took the opportunity to publicly decry the presence and activities of Christian "missionaries" in the land of Israel. When my Israeli colleagues returned from the ceremony, they came as a group into my cubicle on the sales and marketing floor.

"We want to apologize to you," they said.

"What for?" I asked.

"For our government minister," they answered. "He was a disgrace to the whole country today. Your friends won the top prize fairly by their excellence, and they are serving all of us by building our country's technology exports. What our minister said was an embarrassment to all of us, and we want to say that we're sorry!"

By being known as a believing company and by winning the prize for excellence, Ken's company has touched the lives of thousands of working people throughout Israel.

Opportunity International

Often the claims of the gospel are best proved by practical examples of loving our neighbors and helping the poor. Opportunity International is a network of organizations that has adopted a venture capital approach to the alleviation of poverty. These organizations specialize in "micro-lending," that is, the making of small loans, some as little as fifty dollars, to small businesses in the developing world. Thus, Opportunity International's micro-enterprise programs reach out to the poor with low interest loans that are usually outside the scope of traditional lending. Many of the businesses that are helped to become viable are run by one person, often a woman. These tiny businesses can then create multiple job opportunities in impoverished, local environments.

The Opportunity International Network was begun in the 1970s by American and Australian Christian businessmen. Since then, it has expanded globally and helped raise public awareness and acceptance of micro-enterprise as a movement that can spark grassroots, small business development, and impact poverty on a large scale. You can learn more about this exciting and innovative movement by visiting their website: www.opportunity.org.

Overseas Filipino Workers

Overseas businesses have launched hundreds of thousands of Christians into areas as yet unreached by the gospel. Millions of overseas Filipino workers (OFWs) have taken jobs as domestic workers and caregivers in foreign countries. Many tens of thousands of them are Christians who live, work, and minister in closed nations. Even though they do not come as traditional missionaries, they have been persecuted and even killed as they

7

The Joseph Factor

walk out their faith in Islamic countries. In Israel, where there are few believers and a door virtually shut to most missions, the Filipinos have access to homes where they can share the gospel as they serve. Many times, their servant-like attitudes have been a powerful witness to the elderly and their families as they selflessly give of themselves in demonstration of Jesus' love. We have seen Israelis touched by the gospel as they attend the weddings of Filipinos. A few years ago, a young Israeli man approached me who had heard me speak in one of the numerous Filipino congregations in Tel Aviv. He had committed his life to the Lord and is now part of a Messianic congregation. God is certainly using innovative ways to bring people to Him!

These Filipino workers have the capability to impact a nation but they need training. In response to this need, ministries are being established that focus on serving foreign workers in various countries. These ministries connect parts of the Lord's Body in various parts of the world. A network of believing business people in a geographic region or a widely dispersed people group can cooperate to share information, find work opportunities, and locate key personnel. Such a web of relationships can greatly multiply the effectiveness of the participating individuals or group. Regional business and missions conferences may serve to build the strength of the network through training and the growth of new, trustworthy, personal relationships. These gatherings provide a platform for the Lord to impart vision, and for spiritual equipping through training to take place.

The story of Joseph in Egypt has always fascinated me because of its realism. Joseph's story is an inspiration and encouragement to the believing business person who is struggling to succeed both in the church environment and in the world of business. His story demonstrates the important role of the believer in the business world today, and illuminates a pathway to success and fulfillment in both business and ministry. It begins with a family and a promise.

When God called Abraham, Joseph's great-grandfather, to a life of faith, He said,

> *"Go forth from your country, and from your relatives and from your father's house, to the land which I will show you; and I will make you a great nation, and I will bless you, and make your name great; and so you shall be a blessing; and I will bless those who bless you, and the one who curses you I will curse. And **in you all the families of the earth shall be blessed.*** (Genesis 12:1-3)

Abraham is seen by many to have been God's first missionary. From the start, his calling involved leaving his home and being a blessing to all the nations of the world. God repeated His promise after Abraham's faithfulness was tested on the mountain of sacrifice with his son, Isaac. God said, *"And in your seed all the nations of the earth shall be blessed, because you have obeyed My voice"* (Genesis 22:18). Just to make sure there was no chance of being misunderstood, the Lord repeated this same promise to Isaac (see Genesis 26:4) and to his grandson, Jacob.

> *God said to Jacob, "Your descendants shall also be like the dust of the earth, and you will spread out to the west and to the east and to the north and to the south; and **in you and in your descendants shall all the families of the earth be blessed.***" (Genesis 28:14)

Jacob received a new name from God, Israel, and he became the father of twelve sons. These sons were the fathers of the twelve tribes of Israel. What is a family with such a heritage? A chosen family. God had chosen them to be His means of bringing redemption to the entire world. They were God's first mission society. Since there was no other family related by covenant to God, Jacob's sons and their families were chosen and destined to be priests and intercessors—for the entire world. One of the twelve sons was chosen by God for a special purpose. Joseph was selected for favor and distinguished from his brothers. He alone was destined for a double portion of their shared inheritance. He was chosen by God to walk a different path, to foreshadow the Messiah's sacrificial death, Resurrection, and return to His brethren. Through great struggle, Joseph productively resolved the almost unbearable tension of his life.

Years later, his father blessed him saying,

"Joseph is a fruitful bough, a fruitful bough by a spring; its branches run over a wall. The archers bitterly attacked him, and shot at him and harassed him; but his bow remained firm, and his arms were agile, from the hands of the Mighty One of Jacob." (Genesis 49:22-24)

Joseph is a model for the believing business person. Frequently misunderstood and not fully accepted by his brothers in ministry, the Christian business person, like Joseph, must succeed in a hostile, evil, and idolatrous environment. Like Joseph, he must find the courage to watch his own personal dreams die as he embraces the patience to let God resurrect them. He must struggle, often alone, to rise to the top by integrity, wisdom, and the Spirit of God. Like Joseph, the Christian business person must learn to forgive, forget, and press on to success.

Success begins with a dream. Read carefully the following passage from the story of Joseph in the Book of Genesis. It begins with the gift of a father's love and a dream of destiny from God.

> *Now Israel loved Joseph more than all his sons, because he was the son of his old age; and he made him a varicolored tunic. And his brothers saw that their father loved him more than all his brothers; and so they hated him and could not speak to him on friendly terms.* **Then Joseph had a dream, and when he told it to his brothers, they hated him even more.** *And he said to them, "Please listen to this dream which I have had; for behold, we were binding sheaves in the field, and lo, my sheaf rose up and also stood erect; and behold, your sheaves gathered around and bowed down to my sheaf." Then his brothers said to him, "Are you actually going to reign over us? Or are you really going to rule over us?" So they hated him even more for his dreams and for his words.* **Now he had still another dream,** *and related it to his brothers, and said, "Lo, I have had still another dream; and behold, the sun and the moon and eleven stars were bowing down to me." And he related it to his father and to his brothers; and his father rebuked him and said to him, "What is this dream that you have had? Shall I and your mother and your brothers actually come to bow ourselves down before you to the ground?" And his brothers were jealous of him, but his father kept the saying in mind.* (Genesis 37:3-11)

From childhood Joseph was given dreams of authority and great success. He would be a ruler in the midst of his family, one whom they would ultimately honor and even serve. He told his parents and brothers about this dream. Why should he have hidden his dream from them? They were the people closest to him—his whole world as a boy. But Joseph also was selfish and immature. He was probably very proud of his special, multicolored robe even though it made his brothers jealous. The thought that one day he may rule over them caused him to become the object of their anger and hatred. Joseph's brothers sold him to passing slave traders, thinking they would never have to see him again. They reported to their father that he had been killed. Joseph was taken as a slave down to Egypt, but in the eyes of his family, he was dead.

> *Now Joseph had been taken down to Egypt; and Potiphar, an Egyptian officer of Pharaoh, the captain of the bodyguard, bought him from the Ishmaelites, who had taken him down there. And **the Lord was with Joseph, so he became a successful man**. And he was in the house of his master, the Egyptian. Now his master saw that the Lord was with him and how the Lord caused all that he did to prosper in his hand. So **Joseph found favor in his sight**, and became his personal servant; and he made him overseer over his house, and all that he owned he put in his charge.* (Genesis 39:1-4)

Egypt was the world's most powerful kingdom in Joseph's day. Today, the captains of global business wielding the tools of modern technology have eclipsed even some national governments with their power to influence people's daily lives. Business leaders today are the new "Pharaohs" of the world. International financiers control the electronic ebb and flow of vast resources, and they can intimidate the leaders of entire countries. In a real sense, businessmen today are the stewards of modern civilization. Those without money serve those who control it.

In Egypt, Joseph found that the place of his servitude was also a place of temptation and injustice. His master's wife tried to seduce him, but he rejected her advances. The Bible says, *"As she spoke to Joseph day after day, that he did not listen to her to lie beside her, or be with her"* (Genesis 39:10). As a result, she falsely accused him, and he was thrown into prison. Joseph's name means "He will add" and it comes from the Hebrew language root that means to add, increase, or even to surpass. Even in slavery and in prison the gifting that was a part of Joseph's destiny in God was evident, and he became successful—as a model convict.

So Joseph's master took him and put him into the jail, the place where the king's prisoners were confined; and he was there in the jail. **But the Lord was with Joseph and extended kindness to him, and gave him favor in the sight of the chief jailer.** *And the chief jailer committed to Joseph's charge all the prisoners who were in the jail; so that whatever was done there, he was responsible for it. The chief jailer did not supervise anything under Joseph's charge because the Lord was with him;* **and whatever he did, the Lord made to prosper.** *(Genesis 39:20-23)*

Now consider the life of this young man. He came from the one family on Earth chosen by God to bring His blessing to the world. He was the son most favored by his own father in that family. Yet he was betrayed by own brothers and sold into slavery in a foreign land. From a high position of favor with God and men, he ended up at the bottom. In Egypt, Joseph was not only a foreigner and a slave, but also a prison inmate—convicted on a false charge of sexual assault.

Many years passed. Joseph, who was seventeen when he entered Egypt, actually grew up in prison. There was no parole, no letters from home, no hope of escape. He experienced the loss of his loved ones, his freedom and rights, the loss of his future, and his inheritance. His father thought he was deceased and his brothers, who despised him, acted as if he were dead. Perhaps most painful of all, Joseph lost his dream. Proverbs

13:12 says, *"Hope deferred makes the heart sick, but desire fulfilled is a tree of life."* There was no human way for Joseph's desire to ever be fulfilled. Just thinking about his dream must have made Joseph's heart sick. He may have wished that he had never had this dream that resulted in so much trouble with his brothers. The temptation to yield to bitterness must have been almost impossible to resist. I believe that in order to survive, Joseph had to put his former life completely out of his mind. The Egyptian prison for Joseph can be seen as a type of the Cross, a type of death.

However, Joseph had not been forgotten by the Lord. God's gifts and callings are irrevocable as Romans 11 tells us. Joseph learned servanthood by focusing on what he was required to do each day, and he rose to the top wherever he was placed, including the prison system. He even began interpreting dreams for his fellow prisoners. Because of the death of his own dream, it must have pained Joseph to use his special gifting to understand the dreams of others. When Joseph helped the Pharaoh's chief cupbearer, he asked the cupbearer for help in return by mentioning his plight to Pharaoh. Joseph's attempt to change his own situation ended in disappointment. The chief cupbearer forgot all about Joseph's request.

An important spiritual principle is illustrated by the fact that Joseph's own dream became reality through using his special gift to serve and help others. Two years later, Pharaoh had a disturbing dream that no one in his court could interpret. It was then that the chief cupbearer remembered Joseph's unique ability, and so he was called out of prison to stand before Pharaoh. Joseph was thirty years old when this call came. It had been thirteen years since he had been sold into slavery by his brothers.

Then Pharaoh sent and called for Joseph, and they hurriedly brought him out of the dungeon; and when he had shaved himself and changed his clothes, he came to Pharaoh. Pharaoh said to Joseph, "I have had a dream, but no one can interpret it; and I have heard it said about you, that when you hear a dream you can interpret it." **Joseph then answered Pharaoh, saying, "It is not in me; God will give Pharaoh a favorable answer."** (Genesis 41:14-16)

Joseph dressed for success by shaving and changing his clothes. No longer a brash and spoiled adolescent, he was genuinely humble before Pharaoh, saying the answer was only in the hands of God. The mature Joseph was able to interpret Pharaoh's disturbing dream. Moreover, he understood this was God's opportunity to release him from prison.

After telling him what God said would happen in Egypt, Joseph then gave Pharaoh, the most powerful man in the world, a proposal. This presentation was the most important sales pitch of his life.

*Joseph said, "**Now let Pharaoh look for a man discerning and wise, and set him over the land of Egypt.** Let Pharaoh take action to appoint overseers in charge of the land, and let him exact a fifth of the produce of the land of Egypt in the seven years of abundance. Then let them gather all the food of these good years that are coming, and store up the grain for food in the cities under Pharaoh's authority, and let them guard it. And let the food become as a reserve for the land for the seven years of famine which will occur in the land of Egypt, so that the land may not perish during the famine."* (Genesis 41:33-36)

Because God was in it, Pharaoh "bought" Joseph's proposal and action plan. Joseph was appointed to the top operational position. It was an incredible job offer, full of status and authority, a trained staff, job security, and many other extras.

Pharaoh recognized that it was Joseph's spiritual qualifications that were of primary importance.

Now the proposal seemed good to Pharaoh and to all his servants. **Then Pharaoh said to his servants, "Can we find a man like this, in whom is a divine spirit?"** *So Pharaoh said to Joseph, "Since God has informed you of all this, there is no one so discerning and wise as you are. You shall be over my house, and according to your command all my people shall do homage; only in the throne I will be greater than you."* (Genesis 41:37-40)

For Joseph, slavery and prison were his cross. Joseph waited for thirteen years while his own dream of greatness died. Even the memory of his father's house must have filled him with pain, until he forgot about the life and promise he once had. Because Joseph's former life died in prison, his elevation to power in Pharaoh's court was like receiving life from death, a type of resurrection. In a single day, Joseph was transformed from being one of the most powerless people in Egypt to becoming its ruler. He became Finance Minister, Minister of Trade and Industry, Minister of the Interior, Defense Minister, and Prime Minister all at once. The great events of Egypt and Israel began to turn on the axis of Joseph's life, the Hebrew foreigner, rather than upon Pharaoh's. Joseph was God's man, called and chosen from eternity to succeed. Ultimately, the fate of the entire world rested on Joseph's success. He and the brothers whom he saved from starvation were the only heirs of the redemptive line God began when He called their great-grandfather Abraham to a life of faith. Joseph, the slave turned statesman and business manager, saved the "ministry/missionary" family of his father, Jacob (Israel) and thus ensured that one day the gospel would be preached in all the world.

The question of the purpose of suffering in the life of God's chosen people is vividly illustrated in Joseph's life. Why did Joseph's dream have to die in an Egyptian prison for him to realize his potential in life? It is because it was not *his* dream that had to be fulfilled, but God's dream in him. Joseph's entire worldview and his own self-centered nature had to change. Joseph's story is about God's love for the entire world. The core of the gospel is the fact that God sent His own Son to take on the likeness of sinful humanity. In order for Joseph's family to be a blessing to every nation, someone in the family had to be like a person "of the nations." It was Joseph who was chosen to be changed into a man who appeared to be an Egyptian. God's work was so complete that Joseph's own brothers failed to recognize him even when they saw him face to face. When Joseph revealed his identity to his brothers, he did not appear to be like them at all. Sometimes believing business people will not be easily recognized by their brothers in ministry. Kingdom professionals can sometimes look and act like people of the world. We must all learn not to judge only by what our eyes see, but rather to discern the purposes of God as well as the motives and intentions of the human heart.

Another important change had to take place in Joseph before he was ready to rule. He had to forgive his brothers. Bitterness and unforgiveness will destroy anyone, no matter how chosen and gifted. If Joseph had harbored revenge in his heart, he never would have been released to fulfill God's destiny in his life. Perhaps the length of time Joseph stayed in prison had more to do with this change of his heart than anything else. There is a lesson here for believing business people and the ministry family. Because of the high position he attained, and because he had forgiven his brothers, Joseph was able and willing to protect and provide for his family. Remember, Joseph's brothers were the ancestors of Moses, all the prophets, and, generations later, even Jesus and His disciples.

In our day, kingdom professionals are often not considered essential players in God's redemptive work of reaching the world with the gospel. Believing business people have not been accepted as spiritual equals by many in ministry. Joseph's story is a picture of a believing businessman fulfilling an essential calling by caring for the needs of others.

*Then Joseph said to his brothers, "I am Joseph! Is my father still alive?" But his brothers could not answer him, for they were dismayed at his presence. Then Joseph said to his brothers "Please come closer to me." And they came closer. And he said, "I am your brother Joseph, whom you sold into Egypt. And now do not be grieved or angry with yourselves, because you sold me here; for **God sent me before you** to preserve life. For the famine has been in the land these two years, and there are still five years in which there will be neither plowing nor harvesting. And God sent me before you to preserve for you a remnant in the earth, and to keep you alive by a great deliverance. Now, therefore, **it was not you who sent me here, but God**; and He has made me a father to Pharaoh and lord of all his household and ruler over all the land of Egypt."* (Genesis 45:3-8)

As a result of enduring the death of his dream and rising into the fulfillment of God's vision for him, Joseph received a double blessing from God—a double portion of his rightful inheritance. Two sons were born to him in Egypt, and each son's family (or tribe) received a full share in the Promised Land when the children of Israel conquered it under Joshua's leadership. The double portion is a picture of God's success in the life of His chosen man or woman. Joseph's sons represent the two great, God-given victories in Joseph's life: his ability to forgive his brothers and forget their betrayal, and his ability to become as an Egyptian and prosper in that foreign land.

*Now before the year of famine came, two sons were born to Joseph, whom Asenath, the daughter of Potiphera priest of On, bore to him. And Joseph named the firstborn Manasseh, "For," he said, "**God has made me forget all*** *my trouble and all my father's household. " And he named the second Ephraim, "For," he said, "God has made me fruitful in the land of my affliction. "* (Genesis 41:50-52)

Joseph's Success Factors

Joseph succeeded because he was called by God to Egypt. He said to his brothers, *"God sent me before you."* Succeeding in Egypt was his destiny; it was God's redemptive purpose in his life. Egypt is often used in the Bible as a symbol of an unbelieving society which is materialistic, oppressive, and unjust. Just like ordained ministers, believing business people must be sure of God's calling to their particular vocation.

Joseph succeeded because he was able to sacrifice his dream. There will never be more than one way to the Father's best, His perfect will. Jesus said, *"I am the way, the truth and the life. No one comes to the Father but by Me"* (John 14:6. Jesus' way is the way of the Cross. It is when we join with Him in His death and Resurrection that true faith, God's faith, vision, and courage are imparted to our human spirit. Kingdom professionals are no exception to this rule of God's Kingdom. Joseph's dream had to die so that God's dream in him could live. Joseph succeeded because God's Spirit was with him and, as a result, he found favor, and had good understanding (see Proverbs 13:15). Even the unbelievers knew he was different. Pharaoh said to his servants, *"Can we find a man like this, in whom is a divine spirit?"* God's Holy Spirit that brought Joseph out of prison is the same Spirit that raised Jesus from the dead.

Joseph succeeded because he had godly character. He was pure of heart, which he showed by fleeing from the advances of Potiphar's wife even though she was interested in him, was influential, and possibly quite attractive. Joseph showed humility when he confessed to Pharaoh, *"It is not in me; God will give Pharaoh a favorable answer."* Joseph was hardworking and diligent (see Proverbs 10:4) Before he became responsible for the welfare of the nation of Egypt, he had proven himself responsible over the prison system. Finally, Joseph demonstrated that he was a good learner and a dedicated servant. He was willing to do whatever was required and to do it with excellence. He managed the household of his Egyptian master as well as the prison where he was kept. He interpreted the dreams of his fellow prisoners and then became Pharaoh's right-hand man.

I used to think that Joseph's story exemplified a lesson in learning to keep your mouth shut, but it was God's intention for Joseph to tell his dream to the others in his family. How else would a young, Hebrew-speaking man from Israel get into the court of Egypt, the most powerful nation of his day? Joseph's story is an example of how to realize your destiny by going to the Cross and forgiving the ones who put you there! Jesus' parable in Matthew 18:23-35 of the unforgiving servant teaches us about the "prisons" we build through the hardness of our own hearts until we learn the value and power of forgiveness.

It is not wealthy corporations or massive government institutions that will ultimately bring God's purposes to reality. People called by God make decisions and build businesses blessed by Him. We should not be overly impressed with great organizations. In addition, we should not spend our time looking for Pharaohs, that is, great men of position, accomplishment, and stature. We must find our Josephs, whose dreams and visions will bear fruit even if something has to die along the way. We should also identify the fields in which the call of God is greatest. These are our "Egypts." Success will come by matching the Josephs and the Egypts, then praying and letting God work.

Believing business people, functioning as mission pioneers and ministers, are a new paradigm for the Church. Without them, the task of the Great Commission will never be completed. Ministers and clergy have so far failed to release the spiritual potential for ministry latent within the believing business community. As a pastor, I know that many church

PART III

leaders have wanted business people only to serve their own congregations or denominational agendas. We are like the brothers of Joseph. Now we are facing lean years in mission funding, countries closed to traditional missions, and, many times, unwelcoming attitudes toward foreign missionaries by the indigenous believers. Business people, wholly committed to God's purposes, need to come alongside the local believers and help. It is on God's agenda to call out, mobilize, disciple, and train Josephs for the great task of reaching the world before the Lord of the harvest returns.

8

Worship:
THE FOUNDATION FOR
BUSINESS SUCCESS

In the mid-1990s, our congregation on Mount Carmel began to grow and I left my full-time corporate position. The company where I was employed appointed me the director of international marketing. This meant that I was responsible for the company's marketing programs worldwide. However, I sensed the Lord calling me to give more attention to the ever-increasing duties of ministry, so I left my position and registered with the Israeli government as a self-employed businessman. This allows me great flexibility as I follow God's call. I offer consulting services and lecture on cross-cultural business communication. I also teach Christian business people around the world and help to advise Great Commission businesses.

The following section is drawn from my experience in corporate life and my work as a consultant. Far from covering every aspect of the working experience, I concentrate on a few areas of importance not usually covered in conventional books on business success.

The Business of True Worship

Believers in business need to understand the way the world's system works and move its levers of power while maintaining their moral purity and spiritual freedom. That is, they must be in the system but not a part of it.

Jesus prayed to the Father for His disciples,

> *"I do not pray that You should take them out of the world, but that You should keep them from the evil one. They are not of the world, just as I am not of the world. Sanctify them by Your truth. Your word is truth. As You sent Me into the world, I also have sent them into the world."* (John 17:15-18)

A new understanding of worship is essential as the Kingdom of God advances into the marketplace. In the minds of many, worship usually means singing special songs or doing other activities exclusively in church or on Sunday. True worship, that is, God's concept of worship, is much broader and more powerful. True worship is the response of our faith to God's presence. This dynamic of faith, worship, and the presence of God is urgently needed in the marketplace by believers to face the unique challenges and spiritual battles found there. The first mention of the word *worship* in the Bible is found in the Book of Genesis. It is in the context of an intense moral struggle within a family to obey God and make a costly sacrifice. God commanded His friend and covenant partner Abraham to offer his promised son, Isaac, on an altar atop Mount Moriah.

> *So Abraham rose early in the morning and saddled his donkey, and took two of his young men with him, and Isaac his son; and he split the wood for the burnt offering, and arose and went to the place of which God had told him. Then on the third day Abraham lifted his eyes and saw the place afar off. And Abraham said to his young*

*men, "Stay here with the donkey; **the boy and I will go
yonder and worship,** and we will come back to you."*
(Genesis 22:3-5)

The Hebrew word used here for worship is *histachvaya*
and it simply means "bowing down." To bow down means
to submit, yield, surrender, or honor. In Abraham and Isaac's
case it meant bringing a sacrifice. Acceptable sacrifices needed
to be costly and beautiful—without spot or blemish. A friend
of God was supposed to offer God the best he had—his first
fruits. Abraham offered God his son. Worship means giving
God what is valuable, precious, and excellent. Whatever work
you are doing, you do that work for Him, and you decide to do
it in the very best way you possibly can. This is the kind of true
worship that pleases God.

Worship includes singing spiritual songs, praying, Bible
reading, serving, and giving, but it is far more than all of these.
The bowing down of true worship is a decision, a heart attitude
and a lifestyle. John records that Jesus taught directly and
clearly on this important subject. One day Jesus was passing
through Samaria. After sending His disciples on an errand, He
encountered a woman alone by a well. In the conversation that
ensued, He revealed that He knew about her troubled life and
immoral relationships. The woman was very surprised by what
He said and proceeded to ask Jesus a question about worship.

*The woman said to Him, "Sir, I perceive that You are a
prophet. Our fathers worshiped on this mountain, and you
Jews say that in Jerusalem is the place where one ought to
worship." Jesus said to her, "Woman, believe Me, the hour
is coming when you will neither on this mountain, nor in
Jerusalem, worship the Father. You worship what you do
not know; we know what we worship, for salvation is of
the Jews. **But the hour is coming, and now is, when the
true worshipers will worship the Father in spirit and***

truth; for the Father is seeking such to worship Him. God is Spirit, and those who worship Him must worship in spirit and truth." (John 4:19-24)

The Samaritan woman wanted to know which was the correct place to worship—Mt. Gerizim where her people worshiped, or Jerusalem as required by the Jews. Jesus answered her that true worship does not depend on a place nor is it determined by the tradition of any people or by religion. He said that God seeks worshipers who will worship Him in spirit and truth. This means worship from the deepest, most intimate part of our being—our spirit. It also means honestly baring our lives to Him and meeting God in the midst of our unique, unedited reality—in truth. This kind of worship involves the intentions of our hearts as well as the reality of our words and actions. This kind of true worship is radical. It crosses human boundaries, breaks cultural barriers, and creates new borders. True worship from the heart is liberating and fulfilling. This is exactly what is needed by men and women everywhere in the marketplace and other "non-church" environments. We were designed to worship God. When we truly worship, the finest qualities in us are released. Men who worship are truly men in God's image—strong, kind, not intimidated. Worshiping women are beautiful and graceful, that is, filled with beauty and grace from God. The woman at the well had a history of failed marriages, but something in her was restored when Jesus taught her true worship. Psalm 96:9 says, *"Oh, worship the LORD in the beauty of holiness!"* Worshiping God in spirit and in truth restores the beauty of intimacy with God that was lost in the Garden of Eden. God loves our worship. It brings Him pleasure and attracts Him to us. When things go wrong, believers usually start looking desperately for God. We earnestly seek His presence and try to find Him in prayer. But when we truly worship, Jesus taught that God comes looking for us! I think He is better at finding us than we are at finding Him. This is the secret power of true worship.

Extreme Worship

God highly values our worship when it is a sacrifice, when it costs us something to worship. This means that our worship in the marketplace or at home is especially powerful when it is hard or inconvenient to worship. My teenaged son is a skateboarder and I have learned something about extreme sports by observing him. There is something special and exciting about sports that go beyond the edge of the expected, and I think there is something special to God about worship in extreme circumstances. I looked for an example in the Bible of extreme worship and found a man who worshiped after being pushed beyond the limits of normal endurance. Job was a righteous man, but Satan was allowed to viciously attack him. His family was destroyed, his personal finances were decimated, his health was stripped away by the devil, but Job, even when stretched beyond the breaking point, chose to worship God.

*Then Job arose and tore his robe and shaved his head, and **he fell to the ground and worshiped**. And he said: "Naked I came from my mother's womb, And naked shall I return there. The LORD gave, and the LORD has taken away; Blessed be the name of the LORD."*
(Job 1:20-21)

The Book of Job contains more than forty chapters of debate and rich discourse about the nature of God and His relationship to man. However, it was not the debate that turned Job's situation around. It was not the advice of friends or business associates that helped him. It was God who restored him with a two hundred percent return on his investment, and I believe that help was already guaranteed when Job first began worshiping the Lord. Worship is what we must learn to do in times of crisis, stress, war, sickness, crushing pressure, mourning, or great loss. The heart of worship is found at the point of your decision to surrender your situation to God. Job could have become bitter and blamed God, he could have surrendered to depression, he could have become angry, or he could have looked for someone else to blame—but instead, he chose to worship. In the daily battle of today's fiercely competitive business environment, Job's endurance and faith make him a role model for believing business people. Job was tested by the loss of everything he held dear, but in the end, God rewarded him with twice what he had lost and an everlasting place of honor among the heroes of the Bible.

Great Worship

Job's life is a biblical picture of extreme worship in the face of an extreme situation. I also desired to find an example of the kind of worship that turns an ordinary man or woman into a great man or woman of God. Extreme worship is required when someone is pushed over the edge in life, but great worship has a transforming quality to it that can redefine a humble person's destiny. Once again, this is the kind of worship that is not limited to church services. Great worship is found on the battlefield of life.

To find an event that crystallizes our understanding of great worship, we have to look into the life of a great worshiper. David, the son of Jesse, was a great worshiper from his youth. He wrote many of the inspired songs we cherish today. His one desire was to dwell in the house of the Lord all the days of his life. But he was not always a great king in Israel. His rise to power began as a fugitive running from Saul, the reigning king, and the armies of his own nation. David hid among the Philistines, the enemies of his people, and deceived them into thinking he had become a traitor. The Philistine king gave him the city of Ziklag as a hiding place. From that base David raided the Amalekites while the Philistines thought he was raiding Israel. Clearly, he led a dangerous life with enemies on every side. One day, however, it seemed that David made a mistake or, perhaps, the Amalekites were simply fortunate. In any case, they attacked Ziklag while David and his band of followers were out on one of their raiding expeditions.

Now it happened, when David and his men came to Ziklag, on the third day, that the Amalekites had invaded the South and Ziklag, attacked Ziklag and burned it with fire, and had taken captive the women and those who were there, from small to great; they did not kill anyone, but carried them away and went their way. So David and his men came to the city, and there it was, burned with fire; and their wives, their sons, and their daughters had been taken captive. **Then David and the people who were with him lifted up their voices and wept, until they had no more power to weep.** *And David's two wives, Ahinoam the Jezreelitess, and Abigail the widow of Nabal the Carmelite, had been taken captive.* (1 Samuel 30:1-5)

When David and his men returned and found everything and everyone taken by their enemies, they wept. Several hundred battlehardened warriors sat in the dirt and cried bitter tears because they thought they would never see their loved ones again. They were sure that rape, torture, murder, and slavery awaited the people most dear to them, and they were deeply grieved. David's own family was among those lost, but his troubles did not end there. The Bible says that he was also distressed because his followers were blaming him for the disaster and were ready to execute him to soothe their wounded hearts.

Now David was greatly distressed, for the people spoke of stoning him, because the soul of all the people was grieved, every man for his sons and his daughters. **But David strengthened himself in the LORD his God.** *(1 Samuel 30:6)*

How was it that David facing this personal crisis was able *"to strengthen himself in the Lord"*?

> *Then David said to Abiathar the priest, Ahimelech's son, "**Please bring the ephod here to me**." And Abiathar brought the ephod to David. So David inquired of the LORD, saying, "Shall I pursue this troop? Shall I overtake them?" And He answered him, "Pursue, for you shall surely overtake them and without fail recover all."* (1 Samuel 30:7-8)

Facing the loss of everyone close to him and an army of angry men with stones in their hands, David turned to the priest and uttered these incredibly strong words of faith, *"Please bring me the ephod."* The ephod was the garment used when a priest went before the Lord to bow down and inquire of Him. David's prayer was an act of uncommon worship. There in front of men who were accusing him and ready to take his life, he bowed down before God and asked Him for guidance. David could have become angry and lashed out at his accusers, or he could have given in to depression and spiritual paralysis. He could have looked for someone else to blame, but if he had, his story might have ended right there, and David would have been nothing more than a footnote among the kings of Israel. Instead he made a decision to surrender to God, to bow down, to worship. It saved him and his kingdom; and all that was lost, he won back. David rose from his act of worship and convinced his men to follow him again. They tracked the Amalekites down in the desert, ambushed them, and brought all the captives and spoil back to Ziklag.

When it was over, David emerged as a greater man in the eyes of his followers. Before the Amalekites attacked, he was their respected leader, but afterward, he had attained legendary status—kingly status. The turning point was his decision to bow down before God, to worship in the midst of his crisis. Worship, as seen in David's bowing down in the fire of adversity, is what I call "great worship." When the natural man wants to strike back or run away, the act of bowing down has the power to transform us into the image of God himself. The wonderful secret about this kind of great, life-transforming worship is that you do not have to be King David to be this kind of worshiper. You only have to face a great challenge in your life.

Perfect Worship

Beyond the extreme examples of worship and the great moments of bowing down before God, there remains a kind of worship that calls us toward something transcendent, something that shines with the glory of God. This worship entices us because of its perfection and because its beauty seems to lie beyond the reach of humans. What would perfect worship be like? Would it have the power not only to transform us but also to change the world around us?

If perfect worship exists, it can only be found in the life of the perfect worshiper—Jesus, the Son of God. He is the ultimate worshiper, and we must examine His life for a picture of perfect worship. He was never known to have played a musical instrument. For those of us who are not musically gifted this is good news. However, He must have loved music and He sang with the disciples. Jesus is the perfect worshiper because He lived His entire life submitted wholly and powerfully to God. His lifestyle was complete and was characterized by bowing down. This is clearly shown in the events just before He went to the Cross.

> *Then Jesus came with them to a place called Gethsemane, and said to the disciples, "Sit here while I go and pray over there." And He took with Him Peter and the two sons of Zebedee, and He began to be sorrowful and deeply distressed. Then He said to them, "My soul is exceedingly*

sorrowful, even to death. Stay here and watch with Me."
He went a little farther and fell on His face, and prayed,
saying, "O My Father, if it is possible, let this cup pass
from Me; nevertheless, not as I will, but as You will."
(Matthew 26:36-39)

The Bible records that Jesus prayed the same prayer three times to His Father. He asked to be spared the horror of the death that loomed before Him. He foresaw not only the physical torture, but the spiritual crushing that awaited Him as He took upon himself the weight of humanity's sin. In the end, the Father himself would withdraw His comforting presence and Jesus would die alone. The humanity in Jesus cried out for reprieve. The perfect man voiced His desire to live. In praying this way, Jesus spoke for us all and validated forever the human desire to live on this Earth. If you or I were considering the inevitability of an awful death, we would pray in the same way. In His humanity, he wanted to go on preaching and healing, mentoring His disciples, and giving hope to multitudes of followers. Nevertheless, the heart of Jesus was completely submitted to the will of the Father, no matter what that required. He had the perfect life to live and it was made complete through the complete bowing down to God's will.

Here is perfect worship. It is the final, voluntary bowing down of a man to God. This worship reveals the perfect joining of God's will to that of a man's and it completes the picture of worship that began in Genesis, when Abraham took his own son Isaac to the mountain of sacrifice. An incredible spiritual force radiates from Jesus' act of perfect worship that has the power to transform human lives. We are saved by His choice to bow down and by the events that followed that decision. At the dawn of human history, Adam and Eve chose to break away from God's sovereignty. It was the refusal of their hearts to bow down to God that shattered us. The Son of God's decision to bow down on our behalf is what heals us and gives us life.

CHAPTER

9

Integrity of Heart

Jesus' example of perfect worship seems be out of our reach, beyond our ability to attain. It is meant to be that way so we will stretch out in faith and press forward as if to grasp it. We will never fully possess this perfection until we are with Him in eternity. However, in our stretching out to imitate Him, the same power that was in Jesus emanates from us. As we strive to live as He lived and to die as He died, the lives of others around us are impacted. They see Jesus in us and they are transformed. This is the function and glory of His perfect worship. Here are three examples of bowing down to God: extreme, great, and perfect worship. Together they illustrate what I understand to be true worship.

True worship is not just what people do on their Sabbath day. The fact is that true worship is more important at home with your family, in the workplace, or the public eye. These are the places where we most desperately need to model graceful submission to God and to release this power to change lives. The question is not whether we are using the correct religious language or singing the right songs. The real issue is, are we bowing down to God and surrendering to His will in every aspect of our lives? The essence of worship is found in decisions made every day in small ways as well as large—decisions to bow down, surrender, and yield to your heavenly Father. This is true worship and it can take place at any time of the day, whatever your occupation, whenever and wherever you decide to turn your heart toward Him. God's plan is to build a community of worshipers who are disciplined in honoring Him in the marketplace. He desires that the workplace become an environment of spiritual intimacy and union with God rather than a labyrinth of alienation, cutthroat competition, and idolatry. True worship will always mean submitting to God's highest and best will for your life. Thus, finding and following your unique calling is one of the best ways to worship Him. Submit all your decisions to His wisdom. Confess your problems, faults, and sins to Him in prayer. Give thanks for His victories in your life—past, present, and future. Practically speaking, believers in business can begin to worship at work by bowing down to God and bringing Him a sacrifice of excellence every day. This pleases the heart of God and starts the process of sowing seeds of transformation in the business environment.

*Better is the poor who walks in his integrity, than he who is
crooked though he be rich.*
(Proverbs 28:6)

The integration of business and ministry brings us to a
related word: *integrity*. The English word *integrity* is
based on the word *integer* that means a whole number
or a complete unit. Integrity means wholeness and the absence
of dichotomy or a double standard. A person with integrity
is a whole person, an undivided person. This is someone who
is the same person at the office and in church; someone who
is the same person in private as well as in public. Jesus the
Messiah was a person with integrity. He was not two-faced or
fragmented while representing both earthly humanity and His
heavenly Father. He was as good as His word. Whatever He
said privately to His disciples, He accomplished publicly. Jesus
said, *"Heaven and earth will pass away, but My words will by
no means pass away"* (Matthew 24:35).

Another way to view integrity is to consider the way a
civil engineer speaks of a building with "structural integrity."
This kind of integrity keeps the building strong and safe. Flaws
in structural integrity are revealed under pressure or unusual
stress. A few years ago there was a major earthquake in Taiwan.
Many people were killed and injured when the pre-dawn quake
caused hundreds of reinforced concrete buildings to suddenly
collapse. The shattered buildings revealed that some had been
built with large, empty metal cans inserted into columns and
beams where there should have been solid concrete. Structural
integrity had been sacrificed for profit.

How many of our lives have empty spaces where there
should be something solid and strong? When we speak the
Word of God, are we building a house of faith that will stand up
under stress? Believers are people of truth. We should never fear
that speaking the truth in love will cause us to fail. The opposite

is true. We need wisdom regarding how and when to speak the truth. God is the shield of protection for the one whose life is committed to His word. Integrity, however, is more than simply honesty in business. Integrity means keeping our commitments, whether it is a matter between us and God (such as tithing) or in relationships with our fellow human beings. This extends from the contracts we sign to returning telephone calls and being on time for our appointments.

Integrity entails a lifestyle of worship and prayer that undergirds all business and ministry activities. Worshiping God draws us into a place of intimacy with Him. Through genuine worship in God's Spirit, we are transformed into His image and our own flawed character is healed. In our inward, personal life with the Lord, we learn to stand before God and man in honesty. He sends us forth from the holy meeting place of prayer, ready for whatever kind of work our calling entails. Through prayer and the Word of God, we receive wisdom, grace, and moral understanding to deal with tough decisions, to navigate through human complexities, and to avoid moral compromise. Through prayer and the wholeness of integrity, we receive courage from the Spirit to act on what God has shown us to be the right path for our lives.

Achieving a life of integrity means developing one of the basic characteristics of God himself. The Bible teaches that God is one, meaning He is whole, complete. The first prayer learned by nearly every Jewish person is called the *Shema*. It is a recitation of the verse found in Deuteronomy 6:4, *"Hear, O Israel: The LORD our God, the LORD is one!"* Immediately following is the verse, *"You shall love the LORD your God with all your heart, with all your soul, and with all your strength."* This second verse (Deuteronomy 6:5) reveals that the secret of wholeness is found in loving God with all our heart, soul, and strength. Jesus taught that this verse is the first and greatest commandment.

The spirit, which in this verse could be thought of as the

heart, holds our deepest intentions and motives. It is where the Holy Spirit resides. The soul is the seat of our thoughts, will, and emotions. The Greek word for soul is *psuche*, from which we derive the word psychology—the science of the soul. However, the soul is not godly by nature. It can easily be influenced by evil. The Apostle James wrote: *"This wisdom does not descend from above, but is earthly, sensual [psuchikos or soulish], demonic"* (James 3:15). The soul, however, can produce many beautiful and powerful expressions. As a result, many believers live their lives guided by the soul—by their own lofty thoughts, self-disciplined (religious) will, and by their noble and good feelings. The problem is when our soul's human nature encounters satanic opposition, our best thoughts, emotions, and even self-will swiftly desert us. The power of the soul is no match against spiritual evil and sin. Without God's supernatural, spiritual strength, human soul power is easily overcome by the deceit and violence of evil.

Our body is the third component of every human. The body is the seat of basic human instincts, in which physical strength resides, and it frames all human behavior. What we do with our bodies is very important to the Lord. The Book of Proverbs says, *"Even a child is known by his deeds, whether what he does is pure and right"* (Proverbs 20:11). Our words and deeds may be physical acts, but they have eternal consequences. Jesus taught, *"For by your words you will be justified, and by your words you will be condemned"* (Matthew 12:37).

Paul wrote, *"Now may the God of peace Himself sanctify you completely; and may your whole spirit, soul, and body be preserved blameless at the coming of our Lord Jesus Christ"* (1 Thessalonians 5:23). It is the *God of peace* who performs this change in us. His desire is for us to be like Him, that is, whole, complete, at peace within ourselves. The Hebrew word for peace, *shalom*, has the same root as the word for complete. I believe this is what Jesus meant when He said, *"Therefore you shall be perfect, just as your Father in heaven is perfect"* (Matthew 5:48). He could not have meant that God expects us never to make mistakes, to fail, or sin. He meant we are expected to become whole, complete, integrated. The Greek word used here for perfect is *teleios,* and its meaning is fulfillment of God's goal of completion in us.

Someone with integrity is someone who is whole, undivided, and complete. A whole person is the same person in private and public, inside and outside, at home and in church, at rest and in the office. This is biblical integrity. We become people of integrity by the power of God's Word working in our lives and molding our characters by faith. First of all, we need God's Word to clarify the confusion that arises between spirit and soul. Sometimes it is not easy to tell the difference between thoughts or actions that arise from the soul or from the spirit. There is a tendency in most believers to consider our own deeply held feelings or convictions as spiritual and originating with God. This can be a source of deception and danger. Even mature believers are often mistaken. How can we learn to tell the difference? The Bible teaches that God gives us His Word to unerringly guide us. The writer to the Hebrews addresses this in Hebrews 4:12. *"For the word of God is living and powerful, and sharper than any two-edged sword, piercing even to the division of soul and spirit, and of joints and marrow, and is a discerner of the thoughts and intents of the heart."*

God does not send His living Word only to restore our souls or heal our bodies. He speaks His word into our spirit. The wholeness of integrity begins here. Jesus said, *"It is the Spirit who gives life; the flesh profits nothing. The words that I speak to you are spirit, and they are life"* (John 6:63). Transformation begins when God's living Word containing His thoughts and intentions for us penetrate our spirit. Our spirit responds with faith, and God's will begins to dominate our soul's desires and physical longings. When our soul's thoughts and feelings line up with God's Word that speaks to our spirit, our words and behavior also begin to change. This is the process and battle of discipleship. God's Word in our spirit must eventually dominate and control our lives. It is not instantaneous or easy, but is an intense struggle to mature and become whole.

The lives of two Biblical men exemplify this battle. Abraham's grandson Jacob was sensitive, creative, and he craved his father's blessing. His older brother Esau was a strong man, a hunter, and his father's favorite son. Knowing he would never have his own father's favor, Jacob was driven to seek recognition and success in life. He was intensely competitive, and cunningly took advantage of his brother. Jacob manipulated his brother into selling his birthright, then lied to their father and stole his brother's blessing. Jacob was the kind of person who would do almost anything and fight almost anybody in order to succeed. Jacob, however, had been chosen by Almighty God. He received a dream and a heavenly vision. It was a call, a word from God who sovereignly chooses individuals for His own reasons. He is intensely purposeful and always chooses the right person for the right job. There came a day when Jacob had a face-to-face encounter with God himself.

*Then Jacob was left alone; and a Man wrestled with him until the breaking of day. Now when He saw that He did not prevail against him, He touched the socket of his hip; and the socket of Jacob's hip was out of joint as He wrestled with him. And He said, "Let Me go, for the day breaks." But he said, "I will not let You go unless You bless me!" So He said to him, "What is your name?" And he said, "Jacob." And He said, "**Your name shall no longer be called Jacob, but Israel;** for you have struggled with God and with men, and have prevailed." Then Jacob asked, saying, "Tell me Your name, I pray." And He said, "Why is it that you ask about My name?" And He blessed him there. And Jacob called the name of the place Peniel: "For **I have seen God face to face,** and my life is preserved." (Genesis 32: 24-30)*

Jacob struggled with everyone close to him and finally he wrestled with God! He was ultra-ambitious, a striver, and a deceiver until he finally went one-on-one with his Creator. Through struggle and pain he was transformed into a man of integrity—a whole man of faith and the father of a mighty nation. The new name he was given by God, Israel, became the name for God's people throughout generations. God's purposes in choosing us are closely linked to our integrity and our eternal identity.

There are strategic battles in your life of faith from which there is no easy retreat. When we walk with God, we will face daunting conflicts from which there seems to be no escape. Win or lose, if we submit to God and walk through it, He will have His way in us and integrity will be the result.

Another biblical example is found in the life of Peter. He was unreliable, impulsive, boastful, untrustworthy, and weak in character. No one would have believed he would become a man of such personal integrity and spiritual power that his mere shadow would heal and restore afflicted people. The transformation in Peter began during a face-to-face encounter with Jesus and through a word God spoke to his spirit that day.

When Jesus came into the region of Caesarea Philippi, He asked His disciples, saying, "Who do men say that I, the Son of Man, am?" So they said, "Some say John the Baptist, some Elijah, and others Jeremiah or one of the prophets." He said to them, "But who do you say that I am?" Simon Peter answered and said, "You are the Christ, the Son of the living God." Jesus answered and said to him, "Blessed are you, Simon Bar-Jonah, for flesh and blood has not revealed this to you, but My Father who is in heaven. And I also say to you that you are Peter, and on this rock I will build My church, and the gates of Hades shall not prevail against it. And I will give you the keys of the kingdom of heaven, and whatever you bind on earth will be bound in heaven,

Focus
AND SINGLENESS OF MIND

and whatever you loose on earth will be loosed in heaven." (Matthew 16:13-19)

Peter answered Jesus' question and correctly identified the Master as the long awaited Messiah of Israel. Jesus used that occasion as an opportunity to speak prophetically to Peter's spirit. Jesus prophesied Peter's destiny, the identity of his God-given character. God's Word went into his heart, but it still had to be worked out in his life. Later, in Jerusalem, he denied the Lord when the crisis came. He had boasted that he would protect the Lord and then he failed at his point of pride. The Bible says that afterward Peter *wept bitterly*. Following that disillusionment, he quit the ministry and went back to his old profession as a fisherman taking half of the disciples with him. In one of the most moving encounters of the Bible, the resurrected Jesus met him by the Sea of Galilee and restored him.

In the days following his restoration, Peter became a man of rock-like faith and authority. He was a new man characterized by wholeness and integrity. He opened the door of faith to the Jewish people in Jerusalem on the Day of Pentecost and later to the Gentiles at the house of Cornelius in Caesarea. He had the keys to God's Kingdom and used them with authority. He worked miracles, healing the sick, and even raising the dead. Tradition tells us that Peter eventually gave his life as a martyr, sealing his testimony for all time. Peter had emerged from his personal battle with integrity as a man who could be trusted by God to even do miracles!

God creates integrity in ordinary men and women who follow Him by speaking a powerful word of spiritual identity deep in our innermost being. We mature into wholeness as our lives are integrated around this spiritual word in our hearts. Wholeness and integrity are not produced instantaneously. They are the fruit of a faithful life and there is no quick and easy way to ensure them. We receive them by grace and through the death of our old character. God resurrects us, gives us a new name, and a new life. Testing and trials come when we are subjected to stress from conflicting loyalties, peer pressures, intimidation, indecision, fear, and threats of punishment. We are tested by the lusts of our flesh, our personal ambitions, our own dreams and hopes. Each one of us must learn to resist envy, vain fantasies, taking advantage of vulnerable people, selfishness, and self-defeating habits.

The final result of this testing and refining is proven integrity, and an undivided person who can hear the Lord's voice and who is able to do His will. People like this are the builders of God's Kingdom. In Psalm 1, we are told that everything a righteous man does will prosper. Psalm 84 says that God will not hold back anything good from the one who walks uprightly. People of godly integrity will integrate business or government service with ministry and any other calling the Lord intends. They will see not only their own lives transformed, but also the society that surrounds them.

Apart from being a great king and prototype of the Messiah, King David was possibly the world's most successful songwriter. What was his secret? He wrote, *"One thing I have asked from the Lord, that I shall seek: That I may dwell in the house of the Lord all the days of my life, to behold the beauty of the Lord, and to meditate in His temple"* (Psalm 27:4). David was a man after God's heart, and he focused on only one thing—seeking the Lord's presence.

Along with being a great apostle to the Gentiles and a writer of many inspired New Testament epistles, Paul was one of history's most effective cross-cultural communicators. These verses give us insight into what kind of man Paul was. He wrote: *"Brethren, I do not regard myself as having laid hold of it yet;* **but one thing I do:** *forgetting what lies behind and reaching forward to what lies ahead, I press on toward the goal for the prize of the upward call of God in Christ Jesus"* (Philippians 3:13-14).

Both Paul and David had hearts and minds that were focused clearly on their goals. They were single-minded in their pursuit of God's best. Most of us can only do one thing well at a time. If we desire to succeed, we must practice the art of concentrating our gifts, abilities, and attention on the life goal God has chosen for us. Finding that goal is most often the result of persistent prayer, deep reflection, and painful correction. It has to do with identifying the primary inner motivation built into you by your Creator. Bob Buford, a successful entrepreneur and founder of a ministry committed to encouraging business people to find their callings, in his insightful book, *Half Time,* calls this "locating the mainspring."

The spiritual life is like a powerful river. Sometimes the current is deep and strong, but there are places where it is hard to stay in the midstream. Effective navigation of this river requires a disciplined focus on God's guidance and landmarks along the way. Practically speaking, what do I mean by this kind of focus?

Define your long-term and short-term goals with realism and clarity in the light of your calling. As believers, we are not trying to amass wealth here on Earth. We are trying hard to maximize our effectiveness for God's Kingdom and minimize the waste of time and other resources.

Jesus said, "Do not lay up for yourselves treasures upon earth, where moth and rust destroy, and where thieves break in and steal. But lay up for yourselves treasures in heaven, where neither moth nor rust destroys, and where thieves do not break in or steal." (Matthew 6:19-20)

Discover your God-given talents and stay within your circle of expertise. In management, this is called, "sticking to the knitting." Find your niche in the market and seek to fill it through hard work and excellence. Exercise discipline to turn down or refer inappropriate opportunities to others. No one can do everything well. May God show us the one thing, or few things, that we do best. Like Isaac who re-dug the wells of his father Abraham, it is important to develop endurance and persistence. Go back to the same sources again and again as long as they continue to yield. Do not lose interest or give up too soon and do not expect to be successful immediately. It is extremely rare to produce anything really good on the first try. Learn to achieve an initial, acceptable level of success and then work to improve it incrementally for a long time. This will test your dedication and powers of concentration, but the end result is excellence. Toyota Corporation introduced their first small sedan called the Corolla in the 1960s. At the time it was not considered a very desirable car compared to the Volkswagen Beetle, but over the years, Toyota improved the lowly Corolla and built it into the best-selling automobile in history.

Microsoft Corporation introduced their Windows operating system in 1985. At that time it was far behind Apple's Macintosh system, but today, after countless revisions and

11

The Will to Win
AND WORKING HARD

many new releases, Windows is used by the great majority of personal computer users. Focus is being single-minded about the task God has placed at hand. Single-mindedness, however, does not imply extreme rigidity. For the human eye to focus on a moving object, it must adjust itself continually. Our goals are established by God in us through prayer and His Word. We exercise faith to achieve those God-given goals.

> *But let him ask in faith without any doubting, for the one who doubts is like the surf of the sea driven and tossed by the wind. For that man ought not to expect that he will receive anything from the Lord, being a double-minded man, unstable in all his ways.* (James 1:6-8)

Ultimately, focus means keeping the eyes of our heart fixed on Jesus the Messiah who is the perfect image of God. If my strategic goal in life is to be like Him, He will keep me in His perfect peace, no matter what difficulties I may have to face in daily business. Faith focused on God has the power to transform setbacks and failures into improvements in our walk with Him. This is because He has promised never to forsake us or test us beyond our ability to stand. The Lord is the One who gives us our first little bit of faith, and it is He who nurtures it to maturity.

Several years ago, I met a businessman who was the chief executive of a start-up company, but when I read his business card there was no title. I asked him about it and he whispered to me, "Actually, I'm an angel!" I learned that "angels" in the venture-capital community are investors who give a new company seed money before anyone else is ready to invest. Sometimes these angels also help manage the start-up. It struck me that God is like that. He invests in us before anyone can see eternal value in our lives. Then He stays close by to make sure we reach the fruit-bearing stage. Paul wrote, *"For I am confident of this very thing, that He who began a good work in you will perfect it until the day of Christ Jesus"* (Philippians 1:6).

If you are in business, you must have the will to succeed. Paul compared the life of faith to running a race. (See Hebrews 12:1) We are in a competition, not against others but against sin, the flesh, and the devil. Paul said, *"For we wrestle not against flesh and blood, but against principalities, against powers, against the rulers of the darkness of this world, against spiritual wickedness in high places"* (Ephesians 6:12, KJV). Many people would prefer this verse to end after the words *"we wrestle not."* I sometimes tell the story of a believer who wanted to play compassionate, caring tennis. He did not want to make his opponent run or stretch or get tired, so he deliberately lost every game and wound up losing every playing partner too. His partners lost respect for him and no longer wanted to play. When God gives gifts, He wants us to use them— and many times, that means facing conflict and fighting real battles.

Jesus told the following well-known parable of the talents.

*And the one also who had received the one talent came up and said, "Master, I knew you to be a hard man, reaping where you did not sow, and gathering where you scattered no seed. And I was afraid, and went away and hid your talent in the ground. See, you have what is yours." But his master answered and said to him, "You wicked, lazy slave, you knew that I reap where I did not sow, and gather where I scattered no seed. Then you ought to have put my money in the bank, and on my arrival I would have received my money back with interest. Therefore take away the talent from him, and give it to the one who has the ten talents. **For to everyone who has shall more be given, and he will have an abundance; but from the one who does not have, even what he does have shall be taken away.**"* (Matthew 25:24-29)

If you are called by God into business, you have been

called to compete in the marketplace fairly, with courage and endurance. We must demonstrate our faith through good work and not be like the fearful and mistrustful slave with one talent. It is God's will that we be like the slave with ten talents who had an abundance. When your customer or your employer makes money with you on the team, they win and you win. Business is like a game and it is competitive by nature. Furthermore, the Lord can sometimes seem like a hard taskmaster. He knows our capabilities and demands top performance. Being a witness in the marketplace means working hard, trusting God, and letting your light shine. Play fair, but strive for excellence and play to win. When you have won and helped a few others win, tell them about Jesus. They will listen to you because you have won their respect.

Working hard and knowing when to rest is an important part of God's wisdom for kingdom professionals. There is a special joy that can only be found through the discipline of hard work. Some believers think work is cursed because of Adam's fall from grace. It is true that the unredeemed world is condemned to futility, but this is not the destiny of men and women who labor for the Kingdom of God. Ultimately, we are not working for earthly treasure, but for heavenly reward. Paul wrote, *"Whatever you do, do your work heartily, as for the Lord rather than for men, knowing that from the Lord you will receive the reward of the inheritance. It is the Lord Christ whom you serve"* (Colossians 3:23-24).

Many people who do not know the Lord work extremely hard and stay at work after normal working hours. Some reap enormous rewards for their labor. The necessities of life, as well as ambition and the hunger for success, drive people to work overly hard. The Book of Proverbs states, *"A worker's appetite works for him, for his hunger urges him on"* (Proverbs 16:26). Christians know that building God's Kingdom is more important than increasing a company's profits. However, when a man or woman is called by God into the marketplace, hard work

12

Resisting Intimidation

and commitment to the job will bring honor to the Lord. The excellence of God's people in the marketplace must surpass the excellence of the non-believing worker if the message of God's Kingdom is to have an effect in the workplace. Sometimes, by their commitment to working hard on their jobs, nonbelievers put the people of God's Kingdom to shame. I know a successful Christian company president who told me about his troubles with some Christian workers in his company. He said, "It is so difficult to work with believers! Whenever I tell them to do something, they say that I don't love them and they won't obey me!" He was ready to hire more non-Christians because they understood that in order to keep their jobs they had to produce results for the company.

For Christians to succeed in today's marketplace, the value of hard work and excellence must be lifted up in the Church. When asked what he would do if he knew the Lord was returning tomorrow, the renowned reformer Martin Luther said he would go out and plant a tree! He meant that Christians simply cannot sit and wait for the Lord to return. We have an entire world to win for God's glory! A number of influential Christians went on record predicting a major Y2K disaster. This wrong prediction may have been attributed to their underestimation of the amount of hard work that the computer industry professionals would put into replacing outmoded systems around the world in the months leading up to January 1, 2000. Large corporations were driven by the fear of huge lawsuits for Y2K-related problems. They invested billions to fix, upgrade, or simply replace their at-risk software. Today we think they may have spent too much. Many computer programmers worked around the clock for weeks at a time on projects to eliminate the problems or at least provide a quick fix that would avert a total computer shutdown. As a computer industry professional myself, it was embarrassing to think about the non-believing professionals working so hard to avoid a disaster while some of my respected Christian colleagues were predicting one. Sometimes, it seems that people with faith can become out of touch with the working world.

The Bible teaches that *"without faith it is impossible to please God"* (Hebrews 11: 6). The New Testament writer James makes it clear, however, that *"faith without works is useless."* (See James 2:17-20.) Of course, he is writing about salvation, but the same faith that saves us is the faith that sustains our lives. Consequently, when we believe in God to provide our income, our livelihood, in fact, our very next breath, this faith must show its genuine character through our work. If our faith is complete, our work, no matter how humble, will be excellent. In my years in ministry and the business world, I have seen this simple truth proven over and over again—excellence cannot be achieved without the diligence of hard work.

"The soul of a lazy man desires, and has nothing; but the soul of the diligent shall be made rich" (Proverbs 13:4).

Money has the power to intimidate. In the world of business, fortunes can often be won or lost due to factors beyond human control. For some business people, the risks of the marketplace are what make it exciting. For others, the fear of devastating losses can be paralyzing. Ministers can also be intimidated by the power of wealth. It takes money to keep church facilities growing and to fund projects that advance God's Kingdom. Because of this, pastors often find it hard to disciple or bring correction into the lives of business people who are pillars of the congregation. Most spiritual leaders have felt the temptation to grant wealthy individuals special attention and extra privileges in the church. James called this double standard *partiality*.

> *My brethren, do not hold the faith of our Lord Jesus Christ, the Lord of glory, with partiality. For if there should come into your assembly a man with gold rings, in fine apparel, and there should also come in a poor man in filthy clothes, and you pay attention to the one wearing the fine clothes and say to him, "You sit here in a good place," and say to the poor man, "You stand there," or, "Sit here at my footstool," have you not shown partiality among yourselves, and become judges with evil thoughts?* (James 2:1-4)

James' conclusion is we all must practice the same love and mercy toward one another regardless of our net worth and station in life. Love that is fair to all casts out the fear of intimidation (see 1 John 4:18). The answer, then, to the intimidating power of money is to focus on loving people with Jesus' kind of love. The Microsoft billionaire needs the love of God just as much as a penniless drug addict with AIDS. Heaven's question is not who is more valuable, but rather who is ready to receive the saving grace of God? If believers in ministry or in the marketplace are truly servants of God, it will not matter whom He calls us to serve. Money loses its power to intimidate a heart controlled by sacrificial love.

Seeking Acceptance

The desire for acceptance is a very deep human need. It can be intimidating to speak the truth about ourselves with clarity and boldness. Most Christians have experienced the difficulty of telling non-believing business colleagues and friends about personal faith in Jesus and ministry activities. Similarly, when speaking to other ministers, I have felt uncomfortable about sharing my business involvement. Because of the dichotomy in our society between business and ministry, I found that if I spoke to ministers about my business activities, the level of respect they held for me as a full-fledged minister would decrease. I have even been told it is unethical for a pastor to voluntarily support himself through business. At the time, I remember saying, "But what about Paul?" To which the other person replied, "He was an apostle!" Well, he may have been more than just a pastor, but he did write, *"Join in following my example!"* (Philippians 3:17).

Discretion means using wisdom in telling people about your work and what you believe; however, intimidation is something else and definitely not from the Lord. Paul wrote to his disciple and son in the faith, Timothy, *"For God has not given us a spirit of timidity, but of power and love and discipline. Therefore do not be ashamed of the testimony of our Lord"* (2 Timothy 1:7-8a). If a dual calling is your testimony, do not be ashamed of God's unique work in your life. As a businessman and a minister, I usually carry more than one kind of business card in my wallet. There are times when a card with my business identity is more appropriate, and there are other times when I use my minister's card. There are obvious practical reasons for doing this, and in some nations, there are real security concerns. Some of the time, however, the motive behind my choice is to avoid offense or misunderstanding. Of course, we should always exercise wisdom in our dealings with others, but those of us who are called bi-vocationally must guard against intimidation

Building
BUSINESS RELATIONSHIPS

and any pressure to conceal our "other" work.

The Fear of Man
The writer of Proverbs states, *"The fear of man brings a snare, but he who trusts in the LORD will be exalted"* (Proverbs 29:25). There are many believing businessmen and women who are driven by insecurity to seek approval from the people around them instead of seeking God's approval. This is a sad situation because a believer whose life is dedicated to God will never find complete satisfaction in the acceptance of others. There will be a constant striving that never produces contentment. *Workaholics* are people who are addicted to their work to the extent that they cannot rest or feel comfortable apart from their jobs. Too much personal identity is bound up in the job to let it go. This is a "snare" that restricts us, steals our joy, and attacks our spiritual and physical health. If left unchecked, we and those around us will feel the negative impact of this deadly trap. The solution is submitting to the Lord's guidance and accepting His priorities.

We often need to receive guidance and power from God to simply say "No" to a good activity or responsibility that is not God's highest and best for us. God's peace comes to those who through discipline and courage resist intimidation and rely on His grace. The prophet Isaiah wrote, "*The steadfast of mind you will keep in perfect peace, because he trusts in you*" (Isaiah 26:3).

The Power of God's Will

The Kingdom of God is continually advancing into territory claimed by evil spiritual powers. As long as there is sin in the world, there will be an aspect of spiritual warfare in everything we attempt to accomplish for the Lord. Fear and intimidation are evil messengers sent by the enemy of our souls, and we must learn to break their power by walking in the center of God's will. A secret to having supernatural faith and confidence in the Lord is being in the right place at the right time. The right place and the right time is God's chosen place and time for you. We cannot separate God's blessings from His purposes. This means if God wants you in Kiev, you cannot say you are walking in His Spirit and expect His blessings if you are in Los Angeles. The Prophet Jonah is a good example of what happens when we flee from the presence of God and His intentions.

When we walk in the purposes of God, fulfilling our personal calling whether it be in business, ministry, government service, or any other endeavor He has chosen for us, we walk in the power of His indestructible life. Mountains of impossibility must move from our path. God has given us His Spirit so that we will have power, love, and the ability to make right decisions. Scriptures like Romans 8:28 teach us that God has committed His wisdom to turn even the most negative circumstances around for good. The only conditions are that we love Him and are *called according to His purposes*! If God is for us, who can be against us? Fear and intimidation will not remain obstacles for the man or woman of God determined to live in God's will.

Business is an integral part of human life and it flows through networks of human relationships. Effective businessmen are always looking for promising people, even if they are not immediately useful from a business standpoint. When I worked as an international sales manager, I once arrived in Thailand without a single contact. I prayed in my hotel room and felt led to call the commercial officer of a nearby embassy. That person recommended a local businessman with a small company in a closely related field. I met the man and he impressed me as an unusually bright and effective person. In the end, I signed him to be my company's distributor even though his company was not exactly in the best position to help mine. He had about twenty-five employees when I met him, but the next time I visited him, he had two hundred. Soon that figure was over two thousand. One day I heard on the news that he had been appointed to a cabinet level position without any previous government experience at that level. His company became one of the largest and most powerful in its field.

God knows that people make businesses succeed or fail. He will lead us to effective and appropriate people if we follow His guidance. I have been asked if it makes sense to try to work with friends. In my experience, good friendships sometimes develop as a result of good business, but rarely does the reverse happen. In fact, trying to do business simply on the basis of friendship can be one way to destroy or badly damage long-standing and valuable relationships. Of course, there are exceptions to every rule, but profitable business results from providing consistent value to customers through legitimate and ethical means. Trust between those doing business in the context of biblical morality, international law, and accepted business practices is a practical requirement. Friendship is a great benefit but not a necessary factor. Should believers ever be in partnership with nonbelievers? There are many types of partnerships, but equally shared ownership will not work out in the long run. The Bible warns against it. If you are considering entering into an important business deal with a nonbeliever, it is best to cover it in prayer and seek the counsel of someone with whom you have an accountable relationship.

According to the Bible, God created humans in His own image and gave us dominion over the world. Sin destroyed this arrangement through rebellion and selfishness, but God provided a means of redemption through the sacrifice of His Son Jesus. God's original intention for humankind still endures. People are responsible for every material resource on the planet. Right relationship with God means the difference between Heaven and hell. This relationship always has first priority. However, right relationships with the right people can mean success in business. God's Word gives wisdom in choosing people and in building the kind of relationships that will lead us to success.

Managing Cultural Differences

With the rapid globalization of business, a new challenge of building relationships across cultural lines has become commonplace. Cultural issues are business issues in today's multinational marketplace. It is important to recognize cultural differences and deal with them before they become barriers to the growth of your business. Culture is more than language, customs, and favorite foods. The word "culture" comes from the English verb "to cultivate" or "to grow." It is the environment in which we mature. It teaches us our values, what to notice and what to ignore, how to express our feelings, and much more. Like a coral reef, culture has many beautiful and interesting sides. It grows slowly and silently over many generations, providing a protective framework for indigenous inhabitants and enjoyment for visitors. Many times, however, cross-cultural voyagers have found that culture, like coral, is strong and can have very sharp edges. Smart managers in multinational businesses learn to chart the hidden reefs of deep-seated, culturally defined attitudes in order to steer toward the open seas of good communication and good business.

While in Japan, Rita and I helped compile the data for a study conducted by the Ministry of Education comparing the working styles of Japanese and American managers. The study focused on an American company that had successfully set up its operation in Japan. The company was Disneyland. During the years we lived in Tokyo, they built a fabulously profitable theme park in partnership with a Japanese developer. We studied interviews of American managers who had come to Japan to work alongside Japanese contractors to build the park. The Americans found that while decisions took longer to achieve in Japan, there were fewer mistakes made, a higher overall quality was achieved, and generally implementation was faster than in California or Florida. However, there were cases that plainly baffled the people from Disney. In one instance, an American manager was walking through the site with his Japanese counterpart. They were inspecting an attraction that was under construction in the half-finished park. At one point the Japanese manager pointed out that a particular wall needed to be built one meter from where it appeared in the plans. They both checked the blueprints and found there was indeed an obvious error.

The American manager said, "A draftsman at the architectural firm must have made a mistake. Let's have the workmen move the wall."

The Japanese manager agreed that it was a draftsman's error but he said, "No, we can't just move the wall. It has to go back to the design review committee."

"But that will take days!" said the American. And it did, leaving the American frustrated and wondering why.

Today, American companies control a major portion of global business. As leaders, business people from the United States are often criticized by businessmen of other nations. During my years in business in Japan, I often overheard Japanese staffers complaining about Americans. They would say things like, "It's hard to work with them. They make fast decisions and forget about the consequences. They are like cowboys—shooting from the hip! Why can't they be more patient?" Since moving to Israel, I heard Israelis, on many occasions, also complaining about Americans. But they made statements like, "It's hard to work with them. They are so slow moving. Everything has to be by the rules. They are so square! Why can't they be more flexible?" I responded to my Israeli colleagues by telling them, "Wait a minute. Who are you complaining about? The Americans? Just wait until you meet the Japanese!" To myself I thought, "And wait until the Japanese meet you!" The potential for cultural clash was enormous.

In recent years an increasing number of Japanese companies are doing business with Israeli firms. They are finding that the cultural gap is indeed very wide. Japanese managers value consensus in decision-making. There is a Japanese gardening term *nemawashi* that means "root binding." Originally it referred to tying up the roots of a tree to facilitate transplanting it, but now *nemawashi* is universally understood to describe the group decision-making process in a Japanese company. Before a Japanese company will commit to undertake a project, all the key managers must review the project and sign off on their portion of the plan. When top management sees that the middle managers have committed their departments to a project and a planned implementation, they will then sign off and the decision is made. This is one reason why Japanese corporate decisions are often so long in coming. On the other hand, since the project planning is done beforehand, the implementation of the plan is usually very rapid, with fewer costly errors.

I have observed that the approach to planning and spontaneity in Israel is unique to this culture. After high school, every young man and woman is required to serve in the armed forces of the country. The army molds young Israelis. The training, as well as the friendships developed during their time of national service, stay with them throughout their lives. One of the standard military practices taught in the Israeli army is summed up in the Hebrew phrase, *"Ha tochnit hi basis l'shinui"* which means in English "the plan is a basis for change." Every young Israeli field commander is required to make key decisions on the spot, modifying the original battle plan to allow for rapid changes in the tactical situation. This kind of thinking is carried over into the business world, and may be one reason why Israelis are particularly suited for the fast moving world of high technology. It should be easy to see the kinds of problems that Israelis and Japanese have when trying to work together.

However, genuine kingdom professionals potentially have a great advantage when doing business cross-culturally. God's Kingdom is a place of spiritual life, and it has a unique, transcendent culture providing an environment for truth and practical wisdom. The foundation of the culture of God's Kingdom is the character of God himself. If a believing business person has genuinely embraced the higher culture of God's Kingdom, he or she can become "salt" and "light" in the rough and often ethically murky business world by demonstrating compassion, integrity, and justice in dealing with others. The qualities of God's character communicate across cultural barriers in the most amazing way. Nearly everyone recognizes the value of business partners who care about people, keep their production and financial commitments, and don't cut corners on quality. In a multi-cultural environment, if place is given to God's culture, good business based on truth and genuine understanding will very often be the result.

Demonstrating God's culture requires a determined effort to identify wholly with God's choices and His ways of working. In this sense, the Bible is a handbook that teaches us the culture of Heaven. We need to learn a new language of faith and to develop new customs of grace. We need to have a taste for new foods that Jesus said, *"you know not of"* (John 4:32) and to drink the *"pure milk"* of God's Word (1 Peter 2:2). The Bible is not just a book of history and religious laws. It defines an entire way of life for God's people. Under the Covenant of the Law, God gave Israel—His chosen nation—its culture by divine decree. God's purpose was to teach His people heavenly reality. At God's appointed time, Jesus preached about the Kingdom of Heaven and inaugurated a New Covenant that gave Israel's culture a transcendent, spiritual focus available through faith to all peoples. Coming under a New Covenant with God meant a paradigm shift, a cultural revolution for the people of Israel. Paul said that he counted his God-given Jewish heritage as "rubbish" compared to the excellency of knowing the Messiah. This did not mean he was now without a culture or that he was a "cultural chameleon," changing his nature to suit every expediency. Paul wrote that our *"citizenship is in heaven"* (Philippians 3:20).

We stand in the *culture of a kingdom* that cannot be shaken, and therefore believers are able to redeem aspects of earthly culture and adapt them in order to accomplish our King's purposes. However, there are fundamentals of *kingdom culture* that will never be negotiable. Even though Paul was willing to *"become all things to all men"* (1 Corinthians 9:22) in order to bring them the gospel, he would not worship the Roman emperor to save his neck from the executioner's sword. We must not compromise our identity as God's servants as we function in the flow of global business culture. Kingdom professionals are committed to the discipling of all nations, and it is through visible differences in our lives that nations and cultures will be transformed. While we must recognize and respect aspects of the culture in which we live, our prevailing culture must be *kingdom culture.* In this culture we can reach out to build relationships that reflect who we are in Jesus.

14

The Importance
OF NEW BEGINNINGS

The story of many successful businessmen, as well as some of the best-known Bible heroes, is that they failed at least once and had to begin all over again. We should not be afraid to start over. Believers whose faith is rooted in God's character will have strong enough foundations to master the winds and waves of change sweeping the world. In the days ahead, many long-standing traditions and cherished institutions will be swept away, and others will have to be re-invented. The history of the world is building up to its culmination—the end of the age and the return of the Lord. God wants His people to be able to handle great change and not to be intimidated by the challenge of starting again with a new perspective.

Read the words which came to the Prophet Jeremiah from the Lord:

"Arise and go down to the potter's house, and there I will cause you to hear My words." *Then I went down to the potter's house, and there he was, making something at the*

wheel. And the vessel that he made of clay was marred in the hand of the potter; so he made it again into another vessel, as it seemed good to the potter to make. Then the word of the LORD came to me, saying: "O house of Israel, can I not do with you as this potter?" says the LORD. "Look, as the clay is in the potter's hand, so are you in My hand, O house of Israel!" (Jeremiah 18:2-6)

The potter that Jeremiah saw started over with the same clay. He remade it into something new. God says that we are the clay and He is the potter. Can He start over with us? The word "renewal" means becoming new again. New means exactly that—new. Something that was once new, because of the passage of time, cannot remain new. Everything, even good things, become old. Works of God that blessed, healed, and inspired us in the past can become like idols and actually keep us from His perfect will. Jesus came to inaugurate a new covenant and to bring new life through faith in God's Messiah. However, Jesus knew that human nature is such that when presented with the new, people will most often prefer the old.

And He was also telling them a parable: "No one tears a piece of cloth from a new garment and puts it on an old garment; otherwise he will both tear the new, and the piece from the new will not match the old. And no one puts new wine into old wineskins; otherwise the new wine will burst the skins and it will be spilled out, and the skins will be ruined. But new wine must be put into fresh wineskins. And no one, after drinking old wine wishes for new; for he says, 'The old is good enough.'"
(Luke 5:36-39)

Old wineskins are hard, brittle, and become cracked. New wineskins are soft and pliable. They stretch. Jesus meant for us to understand that our lives are like the wineskins in His parable. Our hearts and minds can be either hard or soft. We can be rigid and dogmatic in our faith, or flexible and able to stretch to encompass new ideas. There is a lesson here from the Scriptures: a heart unwilling to change may soon become a heart unable to change. At the time of the Exodus, God hardened Pharaoh's heart against Israel, and it led him into crushing defeat and humiliation.

IBM was once the greatest computer company in the world. It began in the 1940s as one of several companies making early computing machines. In 1964, IBM engineers designed a new type of computer called the System 360. It was the first truly general purpose, mainframe computer on the market, but it meant everything would have to change. IBM customers would be forced to throw away all their old programs and start over. It was a tremendous risk. There was much internal debate at IBM headquarters, but in the end the System 360 was introduced. It was a huge success. The result was that IBM grew to be a giant that dominated the computer industry. By 1965, IBM controlled almost 70 percent of the computer market. By the 1980s, IBM was the most profitable company in the world and rated several times by Fortune magazine as the most admired company in America.

Today, you do not hear so much about IBM. Microsoft and Dell, Hewlett Packard, Cisco Systems and other companies are in the news. Why? One of the reasons is that in the early 1970s, IBM engineers again invented a new type of computer. Once again it meant that IBM and its customers would have to start over again with entirely new operating software and applications. However, the new computer design was thought to be too much of a risk so it was never put on the market. IBM had grown too big and inflexible to make that kind of a radical change. Ten years passed and other companies like Sun Microsystems and Hewlett Packard developed that same invention. As a result, a wave of "downsizing" hit the computer industry as thousands of companies discovered they could meet their computing needs by using groups of smaller computers linked by local area networks instead of big, expensive IBM mainframes. Today, most of the computers that run the Internet are powered by RISC technology, originally invented by IBM. In 1992, IBM stock plummeted to $49 per share from a high of $175 in 1987. IBM lost its commanding lead through the inability and unwillingness to change. In 1993, IBM did what was previously unthinkable and brought in Lou Gerstner, an outsider from the food industry as the new CEO. Since then, he has managed to build up the company's profits again by radically changing its culture—starting over—and by transforming IBM into a software and services organization.

Author Joel Barker has written a fascinating business book on the art and science of anticipating the future. He defines a *paradigm* as a set of rules or boundaries that define how you must behave in order to be successful. In his book entitled *Paradigms,* he makes the observation that new paradigms often surface before the old paradigm has totally run its course. This explains why many great new ideas are initially rejected by successful companies. According to Barker, wristwatches are a prime example of this. The Swiss once dominated the world of watchmaking. They had been craftsmen of fine timepieces for generations, and were experts at producing precision movements made of tiny gears and springs. In the 1960s, when they enjoyed about 90 percent of the world watch market, Swiss researchers were leaders in the development of the quartz crystal watch movement. However, no Swiss watch company could believe it was the watch movement of the future. There were no gears or springs. In fact there were hardly any moving parts. The quartz watch was electronics, not fine craftsmanship, and the Swiss considered it a novelty. An early quartz watch was taken by the Swiss to a trade fair in 1968, where some Japanese watchmakers saw it. The rest is history. The Japanese built that idea into an entire industry. One leading Japanese watch company, Seiko, continuously developed quartz watches that were smaller, used less battery power, and were less and less expensive. They kept better time than the finely crafted Swiss chronometers. Today, most of us wear Japanese-made quartz crystal watches while the market share of the Swiss fell to less than 10 percent.

In the days of the New Testament, Jesus was saying to Israel that change had come and God was looking for people who were willing to be radically different. How much change did God require of Israel?

Read carefully the following passage of Scripture.

Now there was a man of the Pharisees, named Nicodemus, a ruler of the Jews. This man came to Jesus by night and said to Him, "Rabbi, we know that You have come from God as a teacher; for no one can do these signs that You do unless God is with him." Jesus answered and said to him, "Truly, truly, I say to you, unless one is born again he cannot see the kingdom of God." Nicodemus said to Him, "How can a man be born when he is old? He cannot enter a second time into his mother's womb and be born, can he?" (John 3:1-4)

Nicodemus was driven by his own curiosity to discover Jesus' real identity. Coming to Jesus after dark, he was truly perplexed by the answer Jesus gave him. It seemed like the Master was giving him a riddle to solve and Nicodemus' great learning seemed suddenly useless.

Jesus answered, "Truly, truly, I say to you, unless one is born of water and the Spirit he cannot enter into the kingdom of God. That which is born of the flesh is flesh, and that which is born of the Spirit is spirit. Do not be amazed that I said to you, 'You must be born again.' The wind blows where it wishes and you hear the sound of it, but do not know where it comes from and where it is

going; so is everyone who is born of the Spirit." Nicodemus
said to Him, "How can these things be?" Jesus answered
and said to him, "Are you the teacher of Israel and do not
understand these things?" (John 3:5-10)

Evangelical Christians have interpreted being "born again" to mean a change of heart that brings salvation through faith in Jesus. Could it be that Nicodemus heard something else in Jesus' words? Jesus was saying to this elderly man steeped in Jewish culture and learning, a man of stature and a ruler among his people that he would simply have to start all over again like a child. Being *"born of the Spirit"* meant the beginning of a lifestyle characterized by unpredictable change. This was too great a challenge for the Pharisees, the Sadducees, and the other religious or cultural leaders of their day. Simple Galileans, along with former prostitutes and other social outcasts, followed Jesus. It was much easier for them to change. I am sure Nicodemus struggled greatly with Jesus' words before appearing among the disciples at the Lord's grave. I sometimes wonder if I had been Nicodemus, would I have had the courage and wisdom to leave the mold of a comfortable lifestyle and familiar culture to radically change and follow God's leading.

We understand being born again as a one-time experience with God that leads to eternal life. That is but one aspect of this great truth. New life in the Messiah is more than just that. Being born again means being ready for God to do with you whatever is necessary for His purposes today. Eternal life is not simply a one-time contract we signed at the moment we believed; it is a quality of living—an entirely new way of life. Following the Holy Spirit can be frightening and perplexing, uncomfortable and sometimes embarrassing, but it means eternal life to those who accept and embrace God's narrow path. Beginning again means becoming like a child. Jesus himself warned that if we did not become like children we would not be able to enter the Kingdom of God.

At that time the disciples came to Jesus, saying, "Who then *is greatest in the kingdom of heaven?" Then Jesus called a little child to Him, set him in the midst of them, and said, "Assuredly, I say to you, unless you are converted and become as little children, you will by no means enter the kingdom of heaven. **Therefore whoever humbles himself as this little child is the greatest in the kingdom of heaven.**"* (Matthew 18:1-4)

What is the difference between an adult and a child? Only the passage of time. Children are just beginning their lives. They are discovering, learning, and preparing for the future. Adults, full of experience, are planning for the end of their lives. God says, "Be like a child." Have the mind of a beginner embarking on a fresh adventure each day. Be ready to grow and change. The writer of Hebrews referred to following God as a *"new and living way"* (Hebrews 10:20), and Paul wrote, *"Therefore if anyone is in Christ, he is a new creature; the old things passed away; behold, new things have come"* (2 Corinthians 5:17).

In the Kingdom of God, new things do not ever stop flowing because things once new become old. For this reason, believers in business must learn to avoid over-reliance on experience and expertise. We must accept the challenge and risks of the new. The twenty-first century will see acceleration in the rate of change throughout the world. We are living in an information age. In the Book of Daniel, the end times are described as having an increase of knowledge. Secular futurist Alvin Toffler called society's response to unrelenting change, *Future Shock*. Significant change is usually painful. While the world around us experiences greater turmoil, the unchanging nature of God's character and His redemptive plan for the world will provide stability and refuge for multiplied millions. Armed with the confidence of faith, believers will surf the tidal waves of change sweeping our world. One of the functions of God's prophetic Word is to prepare believers for coming seasons of transition as well as to declare the moral and purposeful actions of God.

CHAPTER

15

The Priority of Prayer

Business for the believer is not merely a profession. It is a calling which needs to be established and confirmed in prayer. The word "vocation" has come to mean an occupation, job, or career, but it is from the Latin word *vocare* which simply means "to call." God initiates by calling us to His will. Our response to His beckoning is the foundation of faith needed to receive the Lord's guidance and His blessing of success. A believer called into business has a great advantage because he or she does not wrestle with tough decisions alone—the Lord is there. His name, Emmanuel, means *"God is with us."*

Business people are continually confronted with situations that are ethically gray areas. Yielding to moral compromise is easy. In addition, there is often great pressure exerted by others to compromise for the sake of the group. Through prayer, believers can receive wisdom and deliverance. Joseph in Egypt and Daniel in Babylon are two biblical examples of men who, by prayer and perseverance, overcame evil with integrity and rose to God-ordained positions of wealth and influence. A wise man once said, "There are two types of people in this world. One kind pushes his way through life and the other prays his way through." Which kind are you? A praying person is someone abandoned to the will of God and consciously yielded to God's plans on a daily basis. In my opinion, this attitude and the practice of prayer are absolutely essential business tools for the believing business person.

Praying specific prayers for specific answers helps unravel the complexities of tough business decisions. Within a year of moving to Israel from Japan, I was back in Asia again on business. As my taxi sped along the highway in Seoul, I watched the slate gray Han River through the side window of the car. I was coming from a meeting at Lucky Goldstar's (now called LG Corp.) headquarters building on Yoido Island and I had a decision to make. Two of Korea's well-known *chaebols* wanted the rights to market my company's fiber optic products in their country. It was a good situation to be in, but one that presented dangers as well as opportunities. Both Goldstar and Samsung were demanding exclusivity. If things did not work out, it would take us the better part of a year to extricate ourselves from the agreement and start again. That would be disastrous. In the fast moving world of high technology, a year or even less is an entire generation for certain products. I had to choose the right partner the first time and I had to choose before I left Seoul.

I went back to my hotel and, as I had so often done before, fell on my knees beside the bed. "Oh God, give me your wisdom to know which company is meant to be our partner. Help me to pick the one that will deal fairly with us and keep their commitments. Show me which company will bring us success by taking our technology into many projects throughout this great country." I waited on the Lord and felt His peace coming into my heart. He had called me to this work and I felt the tenseness in my shoulders relax as His presence came into my small hotel room. I was His responsibility. My job was His responsibility. My success or failure was in His hands. He was with me and together we would not fail.

I continued to ponder the decision before me throughout the afternoon. The electronics division of Samsung was stronger in our field, and as a whole, the Samsung group held a dominant position in the Korean market. On the other hand, Goldstar was also a giant industrial conglomerate and had access to several immediate projects. One of their executives had already visited us in Israel, demonstrating real interest and initial commitment. On the whole, I favored Samsung but I still wasn't positive. Did I have the leading of the Lord? I needed confirmation.

When it was later in the day, I called my office in Israel, where it was still morning. My boss got on the line. I explained the situation and my feelings. "Peter, go with Samsung," he said. I hung up. It was the confirmation I needed. Now it was clear. I would call them in the morning. Over the next two years,

Samsung Electronics purchased nearly two million dollars of equipment from my company. Our products were installed in government research facilities, corporate offices, and in every major university campus in Seoul. In the first year of doing business with them, I doubled my sales quota and won our company's "Outstanding Employee" award. Translated from Hebrew, the award certificate read:

"During the current year, Peter has built and developed the Far Eastern market. Peter not only achieved twice his original sales targets, he also laid a solid foundation for further development of this market in the years to come with his characteristic diligence, thoroughness, determination and above all—his good spirit." I was grateful for the award, but did my Israeli employers and colleagues realize that it was not my spirit but the Spirit of the Lord they saw in me? God alone knows the impact for good or evil we have on those who work alongside of us. One thing, however, I do know for certain. It was God, through prayer, who guided my decision to pick the right partner in Korea that year.

PART IV

CHAPTER

16

Image and Idolatry

We are living in the days of restoration when the people of God's Kingdom are reclaiming the marketplace that was given up by the Church in past generations. As believing business people launch out into the Egypts and Babylons of today's business culture, they are the advance guard of the kingdom, moving into areas of the marketplace dominated by the power of modern idols. Victory will not be won without a spiritual battle. Paul wrote, *"For the weapons of our warfare are not of the flesh, but divinely powerful for the destruction of fortresses"* (2 Corinthians 10:4). Just as the people of Israel were led by Joshua into the Promised Land to possess it, so also believing business people must be spiritually strong and courageous to redeem the land of today's business environment. The Apostle John wrote the following, *"We know that we are of God, and that the whole world lies in the power of the evil one. And we know that the Son of God has come, and has given us understanding so that we may know Him who is true; and we are in Him who is true, in His Son Jesus Christ. This is the true God and eternal life. **Little children, guard yourselves from idols**"* (1 John 5: 19-21).

The word for "world" in the Greek language of the New Testament is *kosmos,* which means an orderly arrangement or system of things. We derive the English words "cosmopolitan" and "cosmetic" from this Greek root word. John is saying that the world is under the dominion of the devil, and that believers must be careful of the influence wielded by idols in this world. Idols are images that distract or seduce our attention from focusing on the Living God. When I worked as the director of marketing for a high technology telecommunications firm, I was responsible for advertising and public relations. I learned the power of a company's image in the marketplace. In a very competitive market, there is often little technical difference between the product of one company and that of another. Even though price, delivery, and service agreements were key issues, often the customer's decision to buy from us depended on our image. For this reason, while my company's business was design and manufacturing, we found it necessary to hire other specialized companies whose product was our image. These companies artfully crafted an image for us using advertisements, press releases, personal meetings, and special promotions.

The creation, use, and manipulation of images are obviously not restricted to commercial advertising. Everyone knows that democratic politics today depend on the public image of the politician. Campaign managers, media analysts, and specialists called "spin doctors" have developed the creation and use of political images to a fine art. National governments budget billions of dollars to create ultra-sophisticated weapon systems they hope will never be used in order to project an image of military strength and readiness to enemy and ally alike. The entire entertainment industry is devoted to producing images that people buy and use for pleasure. Images are at the core of how we as humans think; it is impossible to deal with human life without them. The mere act of reading this page means you are capturing a visual image on the retina of your eye that is being processed by your mind. You can also "see" things in your mind that do not exist materially. The word "imaginary" comes from the word "image." You form an image of me from my words, my appearance, and previous knowledge about me. I develop an image of you in the same way. These images tell us important things like whether we should be friends and if we can trust each other in business. Hopefully, your image of me is accurate and vice versa. Moreover, we each have an image of ourselves that we guard and cherish. This complex image can be healthy or greatly deformed. Some areas of psychology deal exclusively with self-perception; we all know people whom we consider to have an erroneous or incomplete self-image.

My point is that human beings are creatures that create, use, and trust images. The Bible says God created us in this way, and that we exist as His images!

> *Then God said, "Let Us make man in Our image, according to Our likeness; let them have dominion over the fish of the sea, over the birds of the air, and over the cattle, over all the earth and over every creeping thing that creeps on the earth." So God created man in His own image; in the image of God He created him; male and female He created them.* (Genesis 1:26-27)

However, sin has twisted and shattered God's image in us. We have lost our connection to the God who created us to be like Him. We ourselves have become empty images, cut off from the Creator who gives those images true meaning and eternal life. Humans were intended to have authority over all life on Earth, but we forfeited our rightful dominion over the creation because of sin. Satan opportunistically uses our plight to deceive and destroy us. His demonic forces of spiritual evil use attractive, worldly images to pull our hearts away from God's plan of redemption.

Idols themselves are without power or life. They are empty images without meaning. However, idols are made to symbolize things that in our flesh we deeply desire, and so we are tempted to follow after them. James, in his epistle, addresses this issue:

"But each one is tempted when he is drawn away by his own desires and enticed. Then, when desire has conceived, it gives birth to sin; and sin, when it is full-grown, brings forth death. Do not be deceived, my beloved brethren." (James 1:14-16)

Because of our weaknesses, all of us fall or stumble over idolatry at one time or another, and some never fully recover. Demonic spirits hide their evil and deadly intent behind culturally sophisticated and seemingly harmless images. In ancient times, people worshiped carved images of wood, stone, and metal. Today, people give themselves to the power of images that are expensive, technologically advanced (computer generated), as well as sensually alluring.

Even images that once were created at the command of God and used for good can become idols. There was a time in Israel's wandering when the people were attacked by poisonous snakes. God's people were being bitten, becoming sick and dying, so Moses sought the Lord for a solution.

Then the LORD said to Moses, "Make a fiery serpent, and set it on a pole; and it shall be that everyone who is bitten, when he looks at it, shall live." So Moses made a bronze serpent, and put it on a pole; and so it was, if a serpent had bitten anyone, when he looked at the bronze serpent, he lived. (Numbers 21:8-9)

The bronze serpent that Moses made was a powerful symbol of God's grace and healing. Even today, physicians use that symbol as a sign of their profession. What happened to the original serpent that Moses made? Seven hundred years after the time of Moses, Hezekiah, the king of Judah, had to destroy the bronze serpent because it had become an idol.

He removed the high places and broke the sacred pillars, cut down the wooden image and broke in pieces the bronze serpent that Moses had made; for until those days the children of Israel burned incense to it, and called it Nehushtan. (2 Kings 18:4)

The creation and use of images is a normal part of human life, and many images are used to serve the purposes of God. Images of beauty and holiness, courage, and moral strength can be used to build godly character and influence people to worship God. On the other hand, there are pornographic, violent, and deceptive images that can addict, destroy healthy personality, and lead to sinful actions. In between the legitimate and spiritually healthy use of images and the obviously dangerous images and their uses, there is a wide variety of morally ambiguous ones. In the ancient city of Athens, Paul found the central marketplace crowded with images that were idols. (See Acts 17.) Spiritual discernment needs to be exercised by believers in business to recognize and resist the influence of idolatry.

The merger of America Online and Time-Warner was announced in January 2000. This merger was just one of several multi-billion dollar business deals in that twelve-month period. It created a company worth more than the annual Gross Domestic Product of many sovereign nations. It brought together brands like AOL, Netscape, CompuServe, *Time* magazine, *People* magazine, Warner Brothers movies, CNN, HBO, EMI records (Beatles, Spice Girls) and a few others. On one hand, it is a picture of globalization in business that in the future will tend to make national identities and borders less important than ever before. On the other hand, the AOL-Time-Warner merger is a picture of the power and financial value of images. What do all their brand names have in common? They each communicate images with a multitude of meanings and a wide spectrum of moral content. The news media, Hollywood, the Internet, and the music industry have something important in common with the artisans around the temple to Artemis that the Apostle Paul encountered in ancient Ephesus. (See Acts 19.) They create images and sell them for a living.

Some time ago I came upon a magazine clipping I had saved from 1992. A top fashion model named Christy Turlington was on the cover of *Forbes* magazine (May, 1992) for making $1.75 million a year. Eight years later, the income for super-model Claudia Schiffer was reported by *Forbes* (March, 2000) to be $9 million a year. The question is not why fees are increasing in the fashion industry, but rather, why are these individuals so highly paid? Millions of people in other parts of the world will not see $90 in a year. Why does Western society reward these women so well for having their pictures taken? The answer is they are made rich for selling their images. Their photographs are a veritable golden image created and delivered to millions of homes by the mass media. Millions of people both young and old around the world are influenced by these images. Models like Claudia Schiffer are not any more or less evil than other people. Their images are simply being used as idols by the spirit of this age. These idols exert intense pressure to conform on young people around the world.

Is it possible that there is a direct spiritual connection between the influence of idols and eating disorders like anorexia nervosa? Eating disorders are very complex psychological problems that are closely associated with depression and low self-esteem. Hundreds of thousands of young women around the world are afflicted with anorexia nervosa. A person with anorexia always feels "fat and ugly." The person becomes convinced that she (or he) is overweight and stops eating normally. Every year thousands die of gradual starvation in the richest countries of the world because of this affliction in the mind. Anorexia nervosa and diseases like it are a feature of cultures obsessed with weight loss, and a generation of people, young and old, who idolize thinness.

Another item in the news is that the complete mapping of human genes has finally been accomplished. Having the complete human genetic map means that for the first time scientists have the basic but full "instruction book" for the physical creation of humans. "Miracle" cures, replacement limbs, organs, and even "designer" children will become possible and a matter of technology and wealth. We will be able to manipulate the physical being of humans as well as many intelligence and personality traits as well. New companies in the United States and elsewhere in the world are hurrying to patent all or portions of the genetic map in order to use them for commercial purposes.

Today the "instructions" for creating different types of humans have come into the hands of humans. Man, who was created in the image of God, will be able to fashion other humans according to his own image and design. We will be able to cure diseases that have resisted medical science for ages. Industry will also be able to construct even more fantastic living idols and market them. King David was prophetically inspired by God's Spirit to write, *"For You formed my inward parts; you covered me in my mother's womb. I will praise You, for I am fearfully and wonderfully made; marvelous are Your works, and that my soul knows very well"* (Psalm 139:13-14). King David knew the human creation was made wonderful by God for the purpose of worship.

*The Apostle Paul wrote: "Professing to be wise, they became the glory of the incorruptible God for an image in the form of corruptible man and of birds and four-footed animals and crawling creatures. Therefore God gave them over in the lusts of their hearts to impurity, so that their bodies would be dishonored among them. For they exchanged the truth of God for a lie, and **worshiped and served the creature rather than the Creator**, who is blessed forever. Amen."* (Romans 1:22-25)

One of the most powerful things believers in business can do is worship God in the marketplace. Scientific discovery and advanced technology together are a double-edged sword that can be used either for the glory of God or for idolatry and evil. Believers are sent into the marketplace as God's ambassadors with a message of hope, salvation and eternal life. Modern Western culture with its talented men, beautiful women, gifted athletes, incredible technology, and great wealth is at a crossroads. The question is whether we will listen to God's Word and worship Him, or be increasingly led by idolatry into deception, lustful desires, and the violence that accompanies greed.

> *Do not love the world nor the things in the world. If anyone loves the world, the love of the Father is not in him. For all that is in the world, the lust of the flesh and the lust of the eyes and the boastful pride of life, is not from the Father, but is from the world. The world is passing away, and also its lusts; but the one who does the will of God lives forever.* (1 John 2:15-17)

Recently, I read about efforts to recover various paintings stolen nearly ten years ago from Boston's Gardner Museum. According to the news reports, the lost canvases were worth an estimated $300 million in today's market. I wonder what makes these old pictures worth so much money? In spite of the enjoyment provided to many by genuine works of art, are they all of such value in a world where there is so much human suffering and death caused by simple poverty? In parts of Africa millions die for the lack of a few dollars' worth of medicine. There are places in the world where the gospel can be preached to an entire village for just a few dollars a month. That is all it takes to support a local evangelist. Should works of art be worth more than the Word of God that can bring eternal life?

The seventeenth century French thinker and mathematician, Blaise Pascal, was also a committed Christian. In his *Pensées*, a collection of thoughts published after his death he wrote, "How vain painting is, exciting admiration by its resemblance to things of which we do not admire the originals!" A number of years ago, a famous Van Gogh oil painting depicting wilted sunflowers was sold for $20 million to a Japanese insurance company. I don't mean to denigrate the important place of art and artists in God's Kingdom, nor am I saying their work should not be well rewarded. Genuine art is powerful and a significant element of human life. It demonstrates the creativity of gifted people, which is an attribute of the eternal God who made the universe. Nevertheless, the extreme valuation of any work of human hands as a "cultural icon" is vanity that amounts to modern idolatry. If you are a Christian with wealth or a surplus of income, rather than collecting art objects, consider creating a fund to support local ministers in poorer countries or to help believing entrepreneurs start businesses to advance God's Kingdom in unreached areas. For those of us called by God to business in these last days, it is increasingly important to keep our attention concentrated on Jesus the Messiah.

Believers can greatly succeed in the world of business, but we must do so without serving the idols of our day. The Prophet Daniel's companions were blessed by God in Babylon when they refused to bow to Nebuchadnezzar's golden idol. There is a spiritual principle that governs the deepest levels of human life. People tend to become like the thing they worship. If we worship the Living God, spiritual life flows into us. If we worship idols, lifelessness is the result.

Read the following inspired words of the Psalmist:

*"Their idols are silver and gold, the work of man's hands. They have mouths, but they cannot speak; they have eyes, but they cannot see; they have ears, but they cannot hear; they have noses, but they cannot smell; they have hands, but they cannot feel; they have feet, but they cannot walk; they cannot make a sound with their throat. **Those***

who make them will become like them, everyone who trusts in them. (Psalm 115:4-8)

Fixing the eyes of our faith on Jesus, the perfect image of God, is the only way to be saved from the deception and spiritual poison of idols. Jesus is the exact representation of God the Father. We are broken and shattered images of God, but He is the image of the Father that all humans were originally meant to be. *"He is the image of the invisible God, the firstborn over all creation"* (Colossians 1:15). The good news for believers in business is that when we resist the temptation of idols in the marketplace and keep worshiping the Lord, wonderful things happen. We are changed, transformed, and perfected by God himself.

*Now the Lord is the Spirit; and where the Spirit of the Lord is, there is liberty. But we all, with unveiled face, beholding as in a mirror the glory of the Lord, are **being transformed into the same image** from glory to glory, just as by the Spirit of the Lord.* (2 Corinthians 3:17-18)

17

Working
WHILE IT IS STILL DAY

The Bible makes it clear that as the return of the Lord approaches, evil will increase. It will become more difficult for Christians to do business in the world. One day, the great markets of the world will be closed to true believers. (See Revelation 13:17.) All commerce will cease as God's judgments come upon the Earth. (See Revelation 18:9-16.) These present times when believers can enter the business world and also work for the Kingdom of God are a window of opportunity that will not always be open. The words of Jesus spoken when He healed the man who was born blind could very well apply to our day. He said, *"We must work the works of Him who sent Me as long as it is day; night is coming when no one can work"* (John 9:4). It is time to prophetically recognize our opportunity and grasp it.

Never before in history has the marketplace held such a place of influence throughout the world. The great debate in the twentieth century over capitalism versus socialism has ended with the collapse of the Soviet Union. In spite of corruption in the business world, the modern corporation has emerged as the strongest and most effective institution in our day. Multinational companies adapt and expand while national governments fall and even traditional family structures crumble. Today, free trade, international industry, and the mass media are creating a worldwide system. Pulitzer Prize winning author, Thomas Friedman, in his book *The Lexus and the Olive Tree* wrote, "Globalization is not just some economic fad, and it is not just a passing trend. It is an international system—the dominant international system that replaced the Cold War system after the fall of the Berlin Wall." The drive for competitiveness in the global economy is forcing transformation of local cultures and eroding the profile of traditional values. Into the widening stream of global business, believing business people are launching out to obey the Lord's Great Commission by spreading the gospel and by being "salt and light" in the essentially amoral environment of the business world. The flow of global business is also providing a means for kingdom professionals to bring the gospel to previously unreached areas.

In the past, the relationship between the Church and the state was the subject of much controversy. Today, business is increasingly predominant as a shaper of modern culture. The debate has shifted. Christians now grapple with questions regarding the integration of ministry and business. Business in the global economy and ministry for the Lord have different goals and require different skills. A tension will always exist between work for material gain and labor for "heavenly treasure," but the example of Jesus' earthly incarnation and sacrificial life connects these two worlds. Kingdom professionals are called to function in tension while maintaining their integrity before God. The good news of the gospel is that by the Spirit and power of Jesus' self-sacrifice working in our lives, believers called into both business and ministry can do so effectively. They do not have to be compromised, fragmented, or become financial failures. Finding the right personal balance of business and ministry is a matter of prayer and determined obedience to the Lord who calls us all to himself.

Business integrated with ministry was the Lord's intention for the earliest churches and part of His original model for all believers. The Bible indicates that the way God's people earn their living by working in the marketplace need not be separate from the way the gospel is brought to society. Recovering this truth in the Church today requires a very different and new way of thinking. The reintegration of business and ministry means breaking down traditional dividing walls, and building up new, stronger foundations. It means radical discipleship for business people and new models for modern missions. The "10/40 Window" is an imaginary rectangle on the globe that extends from West Africa to East Asia, from ten degrees north of the equator to forty degrees north of the equator. The great majority of people who have never heard the gospel live inside this geographic window. Among these least evangelized people groups, there are many nations where missionaries are not welcome. However, in most of these same nations there are numerous openings for qualified believers pursuing a business calling. In order to complete the great, unfinished task of world evangelization, we will need to find creative ways to join business with ministry, and to mobilize an army of kingdom professionals. In so doing, we can recapture the revolutionary quality of the early Church and become a more flexible, effective and Spirit-led movement again.

The power of this movement will be released through heavenly vision and new tactics on Earth. Kingdom professionals are business people who realize that God's expectation of purity and ethical excellence is just as high for them as it is for a person with "Reverend" or "Pastor" before his or her name. This kind of integrity means a walk of brokenness and humility won through perseverance in trials and testing. Often as a businessman I was tempted to compromise, and several times I allowed myself to be led into places and situations where I knew my witness for the Lord was tarnished. It is through the agony of repentance and commitment to change that we are transformed. For the believing businessman this is often a lonely road, and many have turned back before reaching the goal of true discipleship and spiritual fruitfulness. It is through the discipline of confessing our faults and remaining accountable to others that the Christian business person can learn to stand in integrity. All believers need the help of others to remain in the fiery crucible of God's purifying fear.

> *David the Psalmist sang, "The fear of the LORD is clean, enduring forever; the judgments of the LORD are true and righteous altogether. More to be desired are they than gold, yea, than much fine gold; sweeter also than honey and the honeycomb."* (Psalm 19:9-10)

Believing business people serve in the same kingdom as fully supported ministers. We all serve the same King. There should be no tolerance for a double standard of holiness among the Lord's people. Everyone in the Kingdom of God is called to sanctification and spiritual discipline. This is the key to releasing a modern spiritual revolution. If we bring both business and ministry to a new level of radical discipleship, it will trigger exponential growth for the Kingdom of God. The harvest is so great that without this dual revolution of integrated business and ministry and genuine character transformation through discipleship, we will never complete the task that faces our generation. The Lord is calling out to the Church and to the multitudes of believing business people everywhere to accept a new challenge and a greater vision today than previously required. The words of the Bible and the Spirit of God are speaking to the Christian business community about going into the whole world with the Lord's message. There is a growing sense of urgency due to the lateness of our hour in history. God's strategic plan is the salvation and discipling of every nation, and believers in business have an opportunity to play a crucial role in the advancement of God's purposes throughout the world. The business community as a whole is responsible before God for the creation and allocation of worldly wealth. It is a priority in the Kingdom of God to mobilize and encourage believing business people everywhere to participate wholeheartedly in the completion of the Great Commission.

For more information about the author, please visit his website at: www.Gods-Tsunami.com or contact him at:

P.O. Box 7231, Haifa, 31073, Israel
Email: info@Gods-Tsunami.com

Bridge-Logos

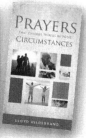

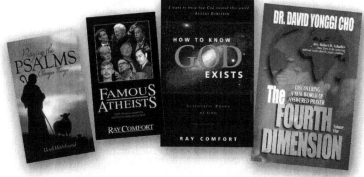

Top 20

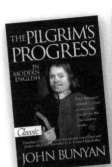

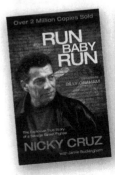

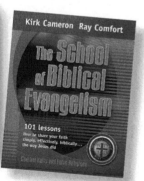

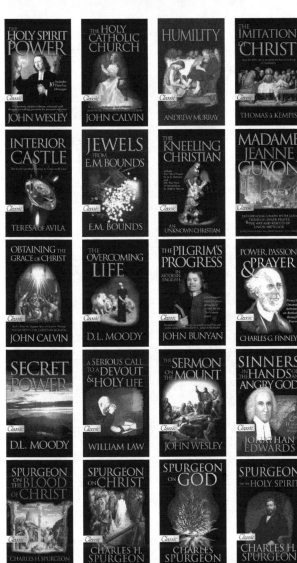

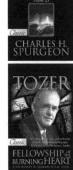

God's Tsunami
by Peter Tsukahira

God's Tsunami is about biblical prophecy and how its fulfillment is joining the destinies of Israel and the nations of the world. The shock waves from this convergence are generating a spiritual tidal wave of change that is affecting all the Earth. God's Tsunami makes prophetic connections for today's Christian reader, connecting current events in the Middle East with God's goal of end-time revival. This book explains why Israel is a nation again today and how the end-time events predicted by Jesus in Matthew 23 and 24 will take place in the very near future.

Understanding Israel and End-time Revival

ISBN: 978-0-88270-984-0
TPB / 192 pages